Contents

The 26th Man

The 26th Man

One Minor Leaguer's Pursuit of a Dream

STEVE FIREOVID

AND

MARK WINEGARDNER

Macmillan Publishing Company   New York
Maxwell Macmillan Canada   Toronto
Maxwell Macmillan International
New York   Oxford   Singapore   Sydney

Macmillan Publishing Company
866 Third Avenue, New York, NY 10022

Maxwell Macmillan Canada, Inc.
1200 Eglinton Avenue East, Suite 200
Don Mills, Ontario M3C 3N1

Macmillan Publishing Company is part of the
Maxwell Communication Group of Companies.

Library of Congress Cataloging-in-Publication Data
Fireovid, Steve.
The twenty-sixth man: one minor leaguer's pursuit of a
dream / Steve Fireovid and Mark Winegardner.
p. cm.
Includes index.
ISBN 0-02-538381-7
1. Fireovid, Steve. 2. Baseball players—United States—
Biography. I. Winegardner, Mark, date. II. Title.
GV865.F435A3 1991   90-27538 CIP
796.357′092—dc20
[B]

Macmillan books are available at special discounts for
bulk purchases for sales promotions, premiums, fund-
raising, or educational use. For details, contact:

Special Sales Director
Macmillan Publishing Company
866 Third Avenue
New York, NY 10022

10 9 8 7 6 5 4 3 2 1
Printed in the United States of America

Acknowledgments

This book became a book, in major part, due to the efforts of Warner Fusselle, the host of ESPN's fine *Major League Baseball Magazine* show. Late in the fall of 1989, I was profiled on one of Warner's shows as the minor league's winningest active pitcher; on the same show, there was a piece on Rick Wolff, a New York book editor who (at the age of 37) had gone back to the minors for a few games with the Class A South Bend White Sox. When I saw the show, I figured the time had come to do something I had always dreamt about: write a diary about one year in the minors. And I figured Rick, as an editor, would at least listen to my dream. So I dialed New York information, traced down Macmillan, and called Rick. What you have in your hands is the result of that phone call, and that television show.

So thanks, Warner Fusselle, for making one of my lifelong dreams come true.

Of course there are other people I want to acknowledge as well. First, the few Indianapolis Indians, especially Scott Anderson, who were aware of the project and who frequently served as reinforcement for an undertaking I often thought overwhelming. Thank you for sharing your thoughts with me, while sparing them from others.

My editor, Rick Wolff, was not only kind enough to receive my words, but went further out on a limb by saying "yes" to the idea. Thank you, Rick, for the direction and stability you provided throughout the season.

Mark Winegardner graciously gave his time and talent to the foreword and made himself accessible to all points in between, all while never seeming inconvenienced by my naivete. I can write, but he is a writer. There is a difference.

John Boles salvaged the modest baseball career I once had and gave me new life with the mediocre one I presently enjoy. He's always simultaneously displayed honesty and compassion—a combination forever locked out to most. It's been my pleasure to have worked for him.

My parents, John and Irene Fireovid, never pushed, never pulled, but always supported. They're a tough act to follow, largely because they're not an act. I am grateful beyond their knowledge.

It hasn't always been easy for my family: Patty, Joey, Sammy, Tommy. Few worthwhile undertakings are ever easy. Please accept this as an apology for the hard times, but even more as a thank-you for the present and future times. Patty, if I believed dedicating books held any merit, I'd certainly offer this to you. I'll dedicate the rest of my life instead.

Finally, ultimately, thank God.

Foreword: A Six-Toed Hero Revisited

Thesis: 1975

In the spring of 1975, Bryan, Ohio—population 7,500, the third-largest town between Toledo and Fort Wayne—was awarded its first fast-food restaurant, a Burger Chef, and its first chain discount store, a Grant City. Both were on the south edge of town, just north of Fountain Grove Cemetery. Grant City, set back two hundred yards from Main Street, had a parking lot that could hold eight hundred cars. There was nothing like it for an hour in any direction. It was a big, black miracle. People came there just to park.

Both chains, Burger Chef and Grant City, long ago went bankrupt, and you probaby haven't heard of Bryan unless you've studied the back of an Etch-A-Sketch or the wrapper of a Dum-Dum sucker: Bryan's chief exports. Bryan now has strip-zoned fast-food and chain stores aplenty on its east and west ends. Then, though, on the threshold of the Bicentennial, when everyone in town drove an American car, those national chains seemed proof that the world was discovering Bryan.

Or maybe I just thought so, since I was at the age where I'd begun to hate my hometown. The idea of a world outside Bryan—a world where, someday, I could live and become a sex-having grown-up was terrifying and irresistible. I was in eighth grade: hormone-throttled, five months and a city block from high school. The snows of 1975 had segued into cold, daily rains, and you couldn't leave a sidewalk without sinking into icy mud.

I'd like to say I followed the Bryan Golden Bears baseball team that year, but I didn't—at least not until everyone else did. Bryan, like most American small towns, valued football first, basketball second, everything else—baseball, track, religion, the arts, ecology, politics, morality, a good ten-cent cigar, you name it—in an infinite-way tie for third.

I knew who Steve Fireovid was, though; in Bryan, Ohio, you sort of know everyone. Fireovid was a fair- and shaggy-haired senior and an all-state basketball player. He went to my church, Trinity Lutheran, on Center Street, and had been in my mother's fourth-grade Sunday school class, in which, according to my mother, he had been a very nice boy.

I didn't know then that he was born with six toes. By the time I learned this, years later, I'd spent most of my life thinking of Steve Fireovid as a mythic creature. His sixth toe was removed at birth, but, after the basketball season, he'd broken the extra bone in his foot and, to keep from stressing the barely healed break, he played third base more often than he did his best position, pitcher. He batted third and hit .442. He pitched one regular-season game and won it. The team entered the state tournament, faced with community indifference, a backlog of rained-out games, and a record of 3–10.

Fireovid pitched both games of the sectional, a three-hitter and, three days later, a six-hitter. Two weeks later, he pitched both games of the district: two underwhelming 5–4 wins, again three days apart. For the most part, Bryan yawned. I can't remember anyone talking about this—or caring. None of the four wins made the front page of the *Bryan Times*.

Then came regionals—four games from a state championship, something Bryan had never won in any sport. Parents, girlfriends, and a few odd jock-sniffers decided to go see what was bound to be the end of a respectable ride. After all, the team was still only 7–10. Fireovid, 5–0, faced the Elgin Comets and their pitcher, a guy named Vern Wireman, who was 11–1.

Forget about it. Fireovid struck out six in seven innings, facing just twenty-two batters, missing a perfect game by only a fifth-inning bloop single. The *Times* sports editor, in a rare display of wit, headlined the story: "Bears Clean Elgin's Clock."

People would have taken notice then, except that the *Times* is an afternoon paper. By the time we learned what was going on, Steve Fireovid, hours after his near-perfect game, was facing the Evergreen Vikings. The Bryan coach recalls that Fireovid approached him before the tournament and asked to pitch every inning of every game. Although Fire doesn't remember making the request, he doesn't dispute the story. Even if he *did* say that, no seventeen-year-old shoulder should be called upon to pitch fourteen innings in two days.

Fire got through the first, three up and three down. In the second, though, the leadoff batter singled. Fire hit the next guy, then got the following two batters to pop up. He gave up a single, then, to Evergreen's catcher. For a moment, this must have looked like the beginning of the end.

In retrospect, it was the end of the beginning. Fire was unhittable the rest of the way, striking out eight, walking one. Bryan won, 11–1; Fire went 3-for-4 at the plate. In the two games, this was his pitching line: 14 IP, 3 H, 1 R, 1 ER, 1 BB, 14 K.

The regional final was broadcast on WBNO (America's first solar-powered radio station, like that's a reason to tune in), and word got around: Bryan's going to state.

Now things got serious.

When the team came back from Lima, a few hundred people were munching Burger Chef burgers and waiting at the Grant City parking lot. Members of the marching band—searching for a bandwagon—grabbed their instruments, climbed into pickup trucks, and followed the team bus up Main Street, playing chorus after chorus of the fight song. They went round and round the courthouse square, like a loud, malfunctioning toy, until the procession ate its own tail and darkness fell and the bus needed gas.

The next week, between rains, high school cheerleaders and batgirls descended upon the downtown businesses, armed with paint and brushes, smearing the windows with golden bears and good-luck wishes. A friend and I sat on benches in the courthouse square, as if we were in church, and watched the girls paint. Their long, straight hair was pulled back from from their faces. They were creatures from another school and another gender, devoted, with ever-more-purple faces, to school and civic pride.

Of course, I knew better than to expect Bryan to win. The next opponent was Medina Buckeye, 20–5, with eight starters batting over .300. Things like state championships didn't happen in places like Bryan, not in my lifetime.

The semifinal, scheduled for Friday in Columbus, was rained out. It rained Saturday, too. On Sunday, the ballplayers—forgiven the finals they'd missed—returned home for graduation. Rain sent everyone into the gym, where a bald Toledo anchorman proclaimed today the first day of the rest of our lives.

The team went back to Columbus. On Monday, attendance at Bryan City schools was a joke. Those who came brought transistor radios. So did the teachers, mostly an army of substitutes. But again it rained.

On Tuesday, even fewer kids came to school. I felt like a nerd to be there, but my parents were strict about school stuff. The game, delayed by rain, didn't get under way until dinnertime. Bryan scored a run in the first, on a walk, a fielder's choice, a stolen base, another fielder's choice, and a throwing error.

That was all they'd need.

Fire threw a three-hitter, striking out seven and walking none, hitting a double and a triple. Bryan won, 4–0.

After the game, WBNO announced that the superintendent of schools would excuse anyone from classes tomorrow who had a note saying they'd gone to watch the state championship.

An hour later, I rode south in a station wagon full of teenagers, stopping along the way in search of a carryout store that would sell us beer. We stayed in a cheap motel, telling lies about girls, chugging Pepsis, and swallowing aspirins until our heads sizzled from the caffeine. We shit in paper bags, set them afire in front of other guests' doors, knocked, and ran like hell. We were excused-from-school boys from Bryan; we couldn't have been prouder. If you didn't hear us, we'd yell a little louder.

By the morning, I just *knew* we'd be state champs. "We"— everyone in town talked like that, like we were playing, like *we* could in any way shape this team's destiny.

In the final game, which pitted Bryan, now 10–10, against Hamilton Badin, 27–7, Bryan's coach decided to start— surprise!—Steve Fireovid, this time on seventeen hours' rest. By now, Fireovid must have thought of himself as invincible. If he didn't, he was the lone Bryanite so afflicted.

Hamilton Badin people must not have gotten excused from school. There were a dozen of us to each of them. We squeezed onto the metal bleachers at Ohio State's baseball field, near the banks of the Olentangy River.

Bryan won a coin toss to be the home team. Fireovid took the mound, and we all stood, roaring our support for the Golden Bears in their sickly greenish uniforms. We stayed on our feet the whole game, following the cheers of shirtless high school boys with orange megaphones, yelling until we tasted blood in our throats.

For five innings, Fireovid was spectacular, striking out seven and walking none. In the sixth, he gave up a single and a double, and the score was tied 1–1. He settled down in the seventh, but so did the Hamilton pitcher. The game went into extra innings.

In the eighth, the wheels came off. Fireovid, obviously tired, gave up a leadoff double. The runner was bunted to third. The next batter doubled. Hamilton 2, Bryan 1.

We tried to show school spirit, but this was what we all, in the pits of our stomachs, had expected. I remember wishing I hadn't come, feeling that my presence was somehow jinxing them. They'd won all the tournament games that I *hadn't* watched. It was all my fault. I considered leaving, just for luck, but I could never have slithered between the sweaty, loud pack of Bryanites.

The fielders seemed to give up, too. The center fielder and the shortstop both made costly errors, and Bryan went into the bottom of the eighth behind 4–1. I really did want to leave.

The Hamilton pitcher, rusty from his long wait in the dugout, walked the first batter. (*Hooray!*)

He struck out the second. (*Oh, no! We knew it.*)

He gave up another walk! (*Ducks on the pond, babe!*)

Fielder's choice. Two outs. Runners on first and second. Now batting: Steve Fireovid. We were hoping against hope, but the sight of our phenom, our seventeen-year-old hero, made the cold logic of the situation fade. (*Rip one, Ste-e-e-eve! Home run ties it up!*)

Well, he just walked, but still. We were hoarse and exhausted, and we believed the simple-minded optimism of our cheers. I stood between two other eighth-graders, girls, cheerleaders in their own right. They each hugged me.

Jeff Grant, the best hitter on the team, 3-for-3 today, stepped to the plate.

Strike one.

Strike two.

Every muscle in my body clenched. I'd memorized "Casey at the Bat" for extra credit in Mr. Spengler's English class. But I banished my doubts, or tried to, screaming another cheer, fearing that my shameful realism would somehow find its way down thirty-four rows of bleachers, over a chain-link fence, and into Jeff Grant's head. I wanted more hugs from Pam and Charlene, man.

(*Rip 'em up, tear 'em up, give 'em hell, Bears!*)

Grant ripped a double to left, scoring two, sending Fireovid to third. Hamilton 4, Bryan 3.

Next up was the shortstop, Dave McCord, who'd also lettered

in basketball and football. He swung at the first pitch, sending
a sharp grounder into the hole at short. Fireovid and Grant
broke for home, heads down, knees high. The Hamilton shortstop looked like he'd get to the ball. He dove.

He missed.

Fireovid scored the tying run; Grant scored the winning run.

Pam and Charlene hugged me and I hugged them back and
we all streamed onto the field, through the gates, and over the
eight-foot fence. The *Times* sports editor would write, "The
Berlin Wall would not have been a problem, as they were behind
the players 5,000 percent and were going to show their love."

We drove home, caravan style, side windows painted purple,
index fingers high. At the county line, a sheriff's car led us
toward Bryan. Fire trucks lined up at the edge of town, sirens
and flashers on. Grant City's parking lot was full, even the
aisles.

The fire trucks led the parade to the courthouse square,
followed by two pickups carrying the pep band and a parade
wagon—donated by the Zenobia Mystics, the local Shriners—
carrying the Class AA State Champion Bryan Golden Bears.

The rest of us rode on farm trailers and trucks, yelling ourselves mute, and it wasn't until years later that I wondered
what the celebration must have been like for the team, for
Fireovid. I rode on a blue Ford pickup, wedged between Charlene and Pam, who, on our tenth trip around the square, each
kissed me full and wet on the lips. Life was new and sweet.
The parade stopped; the high school bandleader led the crowd
in the school's alma mater, which was written to the tune of
"O Christmas Tree": *Bryan High, oh Bryan High/May thy
praises never die.* Near midnight, we went home, weary and
well-hugged, the rest of our lives before us, looming small.

Antithesis: 1985

This story, I'd have thought then, could only turn out one of
two ways. One, my boyhood hero becomes a big league stud,

a Hall of Famer. You know that this never happened; you've probably never heard of Steve Fireovid. Or, my boyhood hero —either because he wasn't talented enough or because he squandered the talent he had—has feet of clay. I confront him years later and find an embittered husk of a man who's unable to deal with a life that peaked too early. That didn't happen either.

That's the problem with sports stories: too often, they have just two possible outcomes. You win or you lose. But a good story—like good art, like life—has a theoretically infinite number of possible outcomes. Steve Fireovid's life—and mine too —would find itself, fifteen intervening years later, where most American lives lie: in that vast plane of human experience between the unalloyed extremes of success and failure.

Here's what happened in the meantime.

Fireovid came back to Bryan that night, unaware, like any schoolboy hero, of precisely what he'd accomplished. What he had on his mind was this: *there's going to be a great party tonight*. And this: *my girlfriend will be waiting*. Instead, he went home to change clothes and never left the house. Waiting for him was Bud Middaugh, the baseball coach from Miami University (the real Miami, the one that was a university thirty-six years before Florida became a state), desperate to sign Fireovid to a letter of intent. The major league draft had been held the day before. Because Fireovid didn't pitch early enough in the season for scouts to see him, he wasn't drafted. Fireovid didn't know what he wanted to do, but Middaugh wouldn't leave. Somewhere around 2 A.M., Fire, exasperated, exhausted, signed the letter and went to bed.

He got drafted after his junior year, in the seventh round, by the San Diego Padres. He made it to Triple-A Hawaii in 1981, at age twenty-four, where he had an ERA of 3.17 in the best hitters' league in baseball, and he got called up to the majors in September. He was a blue-chip prospect; no one could have predicted that he'd spend the next decade in Triple-A. I was a junior then, at Miami University, and I happened to see the box score for his first major league decision. Fireovid allowed just two runs in seven innings but lost to the Giants, 3–0.

Like most baseball publications, like Fireovid himself, I expected him to be a big part of the Padres' 1982 season. He
wasn't, and it was about then that I lost track of him. The next
year, he was traded to the Phillies, a six-toed prospect traded
along with an outfielder named Sixto Lezcano—a quirk I
wouldn't figure out until years later. He came up to Philadelphia in 1984, for just 5 2/3 innings, while his old minor league
teammates—including Eric Show, the best man at his
wedding—were the nucleus of San Diego's first World Series
team.

I got caught up in college, moved to Virginia, lapsed as a
baseball fan, got married, worried about getting into grad
school, worried about getting out of grad school, worried about
becoming a writer, worried about not becoming a writer. In
1985, I went to a ballgame in Baltimore with my wife and some
friends. The Orioles were playing Chicago and the game was
tied 2–2. In the sixth, the scoreboard identified the two pitchers warming up in the White Sox pen: lefty Juan Agosto and
—could it be?—righty Steve Fireovid.

I didn't know how Fire had come to be a White Sock (the
Phillies released him), but I went kind of spaz then, telling
everyone that I'd gone to high school with this guy down there.
That wasn't factual, but it was true. I was an apprentice novelist, just learning the difference.

Fireovid came in. His hair was shorter and he looked heavier.
I started bouncing in my seat, bragging Fire up, and I spilled
beer on my wife. He had an ugly outing, giving up dink singles
galore. The Orioles fans went nuts. I slumped down in my seat,
too disconsolate to keep score.

One of my friends, Dick Bausch—a real novelist—told me
to snap out of it. "It's not like he's your brother," Dick said.
"He's just some guy from a place you used to live."

Synthesis: 1990

The Indianapolis Indians, Montreal's Triple-A farm club, play
their games at decrepit Bush Stadium, which features a hand-

operated scoreboard and a weather-beaten metal tepee beyond the outfield, in a fenced-off triangle of tall grass, snipping off what was once a five-hundred-foot and truly dead center field. The brick outfield wall is sporadically ivied. Like a vacation beard, it's beyond stubble but shy of a full growth. The billboards tout three banks, two insurance companies, an airline, a drugstore chain, a beer, and a soft drink. Only the one for the waffle house ("Round us on your way home!") evokes the tavern and doughnut shop billboards that ring the parks in the low minors.

I live in Cleveland now, where I'm a college professor and a writer with two books under my belt, a third on the way. The time difference between Cleveland and here throws me; Hoosiers, the Luddites, are the only people in the country who don't observe daylight saving time, and I arrive an hour before batting practice. I get my press pass and take a seat behind home plate to watch some kid mow the infield.

I'm here, staying at the Speedway Motel (in the shadow of the Indianapolis Motor Speedway's turn-three bleachers), to meet Steve Fireovid—now a thirty-three-year-old homeowner and father of three—and to see him pitch, tomorrow, for just the third time. I'd called him a few weeks ago in Bryan, the day after his third child was born, to congratulate him and— oh, yeah, by the way—to set up a meeting. *He knew who I was!* He pretended to remember me, which was kind, and he said that he'd seen a review of my last book and that he was eager to read it. "Sure," he said. "I'd love to get together. That'd be great." He spoke in a nasal, guileless, Ohio drawl. He made it sound like he was flattered to hear from me, which hardly seemed likely. "Next time you're in Bryan," he said, "stop by." He'd bought a house on the same street where I grew up.

I said I wanted to see him pitch. What I didn't say is that I suspect I don't have many chances left. He's a thirtysomething finesse pitcher, pitching with his seventh organization, who hasn't been to the big leagues since 1986, when he went 2–0 with Seattle and Topps printed his only major league baseball card.

I'd suspected each year would be his last, but now here he is, still at it, with the best ERA in the league and saddled with the distinction of having more minor league wins, 120, than *any* active pitcher. He's 8–11, a hard-luck pitcher for the worst team in the American Association, a man whose chances of getting back to the majors are impeded by being with the Expos, who probably have more legitimate pitching prospects— Howard Farmer, Chris Nabholz, Mel Rojas, and Brian Barnes head a *long* list—than any team in baseball.

Despite Fire's warmth on the telephone, I have my misgivings about meeting him. For one thing, there's that association with Eric Show. A few years ago, Show was the ringleader of a group of San Diego Padres that got involved with the John Birch Society. Knowing Show was the best man at Fireovid's wedding gives me an uneasy feeling. Even if there's nothing to that, it's still probably a bad idea to meet your heroes, whoever they are, because getting to know them in the flesh reduces them to flesh.

When Indianapolis takes the field, I try to spot Fireovid, guided by only fifteen-year-old memories, a five-year-ago glimpse in Baltimore, and a 1987 baseball card. But I see him, a rangy, loping guy, the first person on the field, running sprints in the outfield grass, then shagging throws from the outfielders.

When the team's done batting, he walks toward the stands, scanning the seats. He spots me and we shake hands. "I'm real sorry," he says. "We have this meeting I have to go to. A lecture about AIDS, I think. This is a good organization; they really seem to care about their players." He shrugs. "After that, it's autograph night. This big promotion, I guess. They let the kids onto the field for a half-hour, and we sign for them."

"That's fine," I say. "Maybe we can talk later."

"No," he says, frowning, deliberate. "I'd really rather talk to you. You've come all this way. From Cleveland? Geez. I'd feel bad if we didn't have time to talk. I'll cut out of the meeting as soon as I can."

We exchange quick, routine pleasantries and shake hands

again. One of his coaches calls to him, and Fire trots down the tunnel.

While I wait, the burglar alarm on Howard Farmer's sports car goes off three times. Each time, the alarm howls for minutes until Farmer—the team's hottest prospect, though he's having a shaky season—is summoned from the lecture to silence his hot, bellowing vehicle. Moments later, Patty Fireovid and her three road-weary sons pull into the stadium parking lot in an '85 Chevy wagon.

Steve Fireovid and I sit at the edge of the dugout, on metal folding chairs, chatting about Bryan, amid the small maelstrom of kids and collectors that makes up autograph night. The prospects—Farmer and outfielder Moises Alou—get the longest lines; if they become stars, their minor league cards will be worth big bucks. But Fireovid gets his share of attention: only a couple other players have had major league cards. He keeps signing that Mariners card with good grace and fine penmanship.

We talk about his season, about his kids, about his intention to retire unless he gets called up this year, about his fear of what he'll do for a living after baseball.

When I mention Show, he becomes more serious. They've lost touch, he says. Fire chooses his words like chess moves. Eric's the kind of guy, he says, who can intellectualize ideas that other people are going to relate to on a gut level. "We'll always be friends, but the communication has slacked off recently. Eric's just . . . Eric," he says, in the resigned tone people usually reserve for ex-spouses.

I bring up 1975 gently. "You guys were 3–10 when the tournament started," I say. "Did you have a clue, even a hope, that you could go all the way?"

Fire begins several sentences before he can find the words. "You know, there was just something about that team," he says. "We were from Bryan, Ohio, and we had these butt-ugly uniforms. We didn't know enough to doubt ourselves. Of all the teams I've been on—" His voice cracks. He signs a dirty cap for a little boy, eyes far away, beyond the center-field tepee and into the past. "Well, there was just something about that team."

I nod. I know what he means. "Athletes usually get asked about how they feel after a big win, right after they've won," I say. "Before it's sunk in. Obviously, winning the state championship's sunk in by now. How do you feel about it now?"

He keeps his eyes on the outfield. "I'd be tempted," he says, "to call it the highlight of my career. But, really, it still hasn't sunk in, in a way." He frowns. "In some ways, you've probably thought about it more than I have. It's not"—he searches for the word—"healthy. It's not healthy for me, now, to think too much about that. I will someday, I guess. But now I have to think about now."

Patty Fireovid offers me another bread stick. The baby fell asleep just as we got to the restaurant. I have a baby boy myself; I know what a stolen moment this is.

"A few years ago," she says, "Steve never would have been able to do this, go out to lunch on a pitching day."

Fire nods. "You could hardly talk to me."

"He was in his own world," she says. "Even more a zombie than he normally is."

"I just have other things to think about now." Fire gestures around the table, at his family. "If anything, I'm the better pitcher for it. I don't think at all now. I pitch better when I'm brain-dead on the mound. You know? Like a machine."

Patty laughs. "Being a machine," she says, "kind of makes him a better person, at least for his family."

Fire rolls his eyes, happy and sheepish, and American dad.

After lunch, we stop to pick up diapers, formula, and New Kids on the Block bubble-gum cards, then go on to Fire's apartment. Tonight is his next-to-last start at home. They've spent the morning cleaning out the apartment and loading stuff into the station wagon. He'll spend the last homestand in a hotel.

Patty, also from Bryan, is two years older than her husband. She was in California in 1975. "I get a kick out of everybody's stories," she says, "and I know how important it is to Steve. This sounds awful, but the state championship doesn't mean that much to me. I wasn't there, and I really didn't know him then."

Joey and Sammy Fireovid change into well-worn Indianapolis Indians uniforms, holes at their knees, random grass stains everywhere. They pull on their caps and mitts, pounding their fists into the pockets. Then they take turns sliding into the couch, until their father emerges from the bathroom, his contact lenses in place, and scoops them up, telling them to straighten up and fly right.

"Steve told me once," Patty says, diapering the baby, "that winning the state championship was the most exciting thing that ever happened to him."

Fire looks embarrassed. "Well," he says. "I guess it was. I mean, I can't really explain it, but I guess it was."

Patty grins. "More exciting than seeing your sons born?"

"You can't compare—" he says, stammering, bouncing Sammy on his knee. Then Fire laughs and looks at me. "That's a loaded question if I ever heard one."

Fifteen years since I last saw Steve Fireovid win a game, I see him win another. This time, he doesn't have his best stuff, although the Indians' pitching coach will later tell me that Fire threw three pitches at 90 miles per hour. He pitches seven innings, gives up four runs, strikes out three and, as usual, walks nobody. The Indians win, 5–4.

In the second inning, I get to see a flash of the past. Fire, a .442 hitter in high school, loops a fading fly ball into deep right field. It hits the foul line, and goes for a two-run double. Two batters later, Moises Alou also doubles, scoring Fireovid with what turns out to be the winning run.

Joey and Sammy Fireovid meet their father in the clubhouse. They're the only children there, and, at five and seven, they're as close in age to some of the players as those players are to Joey and Sammy's dad.

While I wait, I ask the coaching staff about Fireovid, about his season. They can't say enough. "He'll make a hell of a pitching coach someday," says Joe Kerrigan, the pitching coach.

"He makes everybody around him better," says the manager, Tim Johnson. "I wish I had twenty-five Steve Fireovids."

I ask them what makes a player get labeled a Triple-A ballplayer, what keeps a guy like Steve Fireovid from ever getting a long look in the big leagues.

The coaches shrug. It just happens to some guys, they tell me. Who can say why?

"I stunk," Fire says, dressed and smiling. "But I'll take it. I haven't had many breaks this year." He does a polite interview with a writer from the *Indianapolis Star*, then loops his long arms around the shoulders of his boys and takes off.

In the darkened parking lot, he meets Patty and the baby—Thomas John, though they've taken to calling him Buggins—in the station wagon. She doesn't critique his performance, any more than anyone would analyze a spouse's day at the office. Joey and Sammy are keyed up about their father's win, about his hit, and unaware, surely, that this may be one of the last wins he'll ever get. Patty's concern, now, is settling everyone down, getting everyone to sleep, moving everyone home to Bryan.

I stand on the blacktop, watching another man's family behave typically, randomly, like any family: a ballplayer's family, a banker's family, a writer's family. I think about the anxiety that creeps into Fire's voice when he mentions the job search that looms before him this fall. I'd never appreciated how lucky I am to have a career where you don't need to retire, how Fire, five years older than me and writing a book himself, covets just such a career.

I shake hands with everyone and say good-bye. I could, of course, return here Labor Day weekend, to watch Fire's last start of the season. I tell him I might, but I won't. I can't, because if this is his last season, then that will be his last start ever.

The Fireovids' station wagon heads toward the highway, and

I follow. Bush Stadium's parking lot is at least as big as Grant City's, and I feel happy—and old, like a grown-up, if only by dint of allowing my boyhood hero his humanity—to be following Steve Fireovid, one last triumphant time, in a procession, however small, away from a darkened ballpark and into a moonlit and uncertain night.

MARK WINEGARDNER

November 1, 1990
  Cleveland, Ohio

Editor's Note

Everything that follows was written—longhand and pains-takingly—by Steve Fireovid during the spring and summer of 1990. This is no dumb-jock as-told-to book. The editing done here consisted of subtraction, not addition; configuration, not creation; pruning, not fertilizing.

MARK WINEGARDNER

March

Friday, March 9
Bryan, Ohio

Tonight I said good-bye to my family. We went out to Kaufman's, the best restaurant in town—which I don't say just because Patty's parents own it. Patty's five months pregnant now. Joey's in kindergarten and Sammy's in preschool. We joked during dinner about them all coming down over spring break. Guys in minor league camps don't draw a salary during spring training, so flying my family to Florida is a ridiculous notion.

My off-season job this year was at a place called Tru-Fast, which makes roofing fasteners. I manned machine number seven. The days were long, numbing, and sweaty. Patty said I came home smelling like a sour dishrag. The winter before this, I was thinking about quitting baseball, and I interviewed at Tru-Fast for a sales job. I got it. They started me in the shop, teaching me the business, and I worked my way up into the office. I got used to being home every night for dinner. The Royals wanted me back in '89, though, and I went, vowing that I'd get back to the big leagues or retire. I had Tru-Fast's blessings.

I went to minor league camp last year, for the first time ever.

3

I've spent most of my career in the minors, but I at least always went to big league camp. Minor league camp was quite a come-down: cafeteria food, no paycheck, no car, hundreds of twenty-year-olds in the rooms above, below, and beside me. I adjusted, though. A player like me becomes an expert at adjusting. I stayed healthy and, for the second straight year, led the Omaha Royals in wins, with thirteen, which also tied me for the league lead. I won ten of my last thirteen decisions and was pitching better than I ever had. We won our division and faced Indianapolis in the playoffs. I turned in a strong, complete-game victory against the eventual champions. After we were eliminated in Omaha, I was called into manager Sal Rendes's office by John Boles, then the Royals' minor league director. Boles and I go back to 1985, when he was my manager in Buffalo, in the White Sox system, and it was Boles who gave me a second chance in baseball back in '87, after the Blue Jays released me and I was out of the game, playing softball for my father-in-law's restaurant and feeling sorry for myself.

"Go home and stay by the phone," John told me. "You're one of our four top starters in this organization right now. Keep running and keep throwing when you get home. What I'd like to see them do is go with a rotation of Saberhagen, Gubicza, Gordon, and Fireovid."

"Okay," I said. I appreciated the vote of confidence. But I wasn't exactly doing handsprings. I knew John's recommendation would be taken seriously, but I also knew it wasn't his decision, that my fate rested in the hands of John Schuerholz, the general manager, and John Wathan, the manager.

I went into the clubhouse and saw another grizzled veteran, Nick Capra, smiling at me. "What'd they say?" he asked. I told him and we both laughed. He knew as well as I did it wasn't likely to happen. I went home; I was so sure they wouldn't call that I let my boys pack my gear away for the winter. Kansas City's season ended and the call, of course, never did come.

I went to work for the Bryan Parks and Recreation Department, at least until it got too cold to plant trees. Then I went back to Tru-Fast.

Saturday, March 10
Bryan, Ohio

In an hour, I'll get on a plane in Toledo and leave for my twelfth spring training, my second in a row at minor-league camp. I'm now with my seventh organization. My basement-stairway walls scarcely have room for all the winter ball, major, and minor league caps I've worn. Since I signed my first pro contract, in 1978, I've moved forty-four times. I've had thirty-four addresses, twenty-five since I've been married to Patty. I'm a thirty-two-year-old father of two—and counting. I've pitched 64⅔ big-league innings.

And I'm a turd. There are a lot of us, experienced guys stuck at Triple-A as insurance policies, hired to display good work habits to the bonus babies. Sometimes we get called "organizational ballplayers." I prefer "turd."

A lot of us turds are being groomed as coaches. I know I am; it's entirely possible that I'll be asked to be a coach again this year. But I'm not going to be a coach. I don't know if I'd be any good. The thing that eats at me now, as a player, is how much time I spend separated from my family. I feel guilty about it, and I worry that I'm being selfish, that I'm indulging some stupid boyhood dream at my family's expense.

I don't feel that way all the time, though. I'm good at what I do. I believe I belong in the big leagues. That's neither a boast nor a whine. I've only been given six major league starts; my ERA in those games is under three. I'm a better pitcher now than I was back when I made the radar gun dance, and I'm confident I'd be a successful pitcher up there, in somebody's rotation. If I didn't think so, I wouldn't be leaving home.

I've tried to get the house in order, as much as possible, before I leave. I'm an organized person—sometimes Patty would say *too* organized—but I'm not all that handy. My household contributions usually consist of making the beds and tidying up. Still, I cleaned up the basement and garage and poured as many eighty-pound bags of salt into the water softener as I could. Patty's brother lives next door, and it gives me some peace of mind to know that he'll help look after everyone.

Patty and I haven't talked much about my imminent departure, especially in front of Joey and Sammy. We don't want them to be watching the calendar, counting down the days until Dad leaves. That's just what I've done, though.

I could have re-signed with the Royals this past winter, but I felt that would crush any chance I have of returning to the big leagues. They just signed free agents Mark Davis and Storm Davis. The Expos seem a little more wide open; they lost starters Mark Langston, Bryn Smith, and Pascual Perez to free agency. They're bringing dozens of journeyman pitchers to camp. If they think Joaquin Andujar can still pitch, then maybe I really do have a chance to get back up.

I should also say that I'm with the Expos now because John Boles is. He's their new field coordinator, which means that he's basically in charge of hiring and firing the coaching staff. The Expos were my only other offer. Montreal, of course, wanted me because they needed a starter in Indianapolis, not so they could receive any production at the major league level. I'm the only one who has visions otherwise.

But the major league owners are about to put a lockout into place. And the minor league camps open tomorrow. This might not be a big advantage for me. But it can't hurt.

Whatever happens, Patty and I have discussed my future and we've come to a decision. I won't be in this position next year. Unless I can establish myself in the big leagues this year, I'm going to quit.

Sunday, March 11
West Palm Beach

Patty had to deal with a plumbing leak today, not that I'd have been a huge help. I would have been there to dial the plumber. Still, it seems like circumstances always conspire to make her months as a single parent even more difficult than they'd be already.

I had to call home from the lobby because the phones in the players' rooms have been disconnected from outgoing calls. I understand why the hotel did this; apparently in years past some of the kids left and "forgot" to pay their phone bills. But it's an unfortunate inconvenience for a grown-up to endure.

The Country Squire is not a major league hotel, although any hotel, no matter how nice, would be lowered to a minor league standard if you packed it full of 150 frenzied minor league kids. Still, my accommodations could be worse. Most guys have three to a room, sleeping on two beds and a cot. Because I'm a veteran, I've been rewarded with only one roommate, and he's not coming until the infielders and outfielders report.

We had our first workout today. I stay in shape all winter, running five miles a day and pitching in whatever school gyms I can use. But not everyone reports in good shape. Pitchers, in particular, complain in direct proportion to the amount of running they're asked to do.

We spent most of our time standing in line at various "stations," each of which is dedicated to working on some particular skill. The one that threw me was bunting. I haven't been with a National League team since 1984. I was a stranger in a strange land.

Monday, March 12
West Palm Beach

The major league players are now officially locked out. Arbitration seems to be the main issue. Opening day's in jeopardy. The lost time is particularly a problem with a team like Montreal, which (unlike, say, the Mets or the Athletics) has a lot of roster spots up for grabs. After you've been in this game a while, though, you don't waste much time speculating about what all this means for you. You just do that which you can control; you go out and play ball and trust justice to prevail.

I worked off the mound again today, and my arm feels better than it has since '85. Last year at this time, I couldn't even throw. It's fun to step on the rubber and know that, if I want, I can cut loose. I don't take my health for granted, though. Each pitch I throw could be my last.

You'd swear a lot of these kids don't trust the team to feed them. The cafeteria opens at five. The guys start lining up a half-hour ahead of time. By five, there's fifty kids waiting, each with this hungry and vaguely panicky look in his eyes.

Tuesday, March 13
West Palm Beach

There's a lot of time to kill here. I spend hours reading and taking walks, but when I get *real* bored, I count the "awesomes." Without a doubt, the most abused word around young ballplayers is "awesome." The general public gave the word a workout in the '80s, but that's nothing compared to the way ballplayers use it. Already today, I've heard it thirty-seven times. I haven't gone to dinner yet, either. Dinner's prime awesome-gathering time because the guys have had a whole day to experience the world's awesomeness.

Every person, action, or thing here has the potential of being deemed awesome. One player today reported that his room had been blessed with an awesome air conditioner. Another has an awesome shower. One guy was adorned with an awesome necklace, and his roommate has new underwear that's so awesome he wore it over his jock. The younger guys patronize each other by complimenting each other's awesome stuff—fastball, forkball, slider, whatever.

I've used the word, too. The Grand Canyon is awesome. Niagara Falls is awesome. Steve Carlton's slider might have bordered on awesome.

There are no Steve Carltons here.

Wednesday, March 14
West Palm Beach

The Expos' minor league facility must have seen better days. The warning track's full of potholes and divots, and the whole place is more than a little dog-eared. Not only that, it's a fifteen-minute drive from the Country Squire Hotel. We're bused to and from there every day, and the bus keeps getting flats. This can't be a good omen.

The position players get in today and report for workouts tomorrow. They'll be a welcome addition. The pitcher-only workouts are getting stale. Everyone today, knowing this was the last such workout, just went through the motions. Everyone, that is, but Triple-A pitching coach Joe Kerrigan. Somebody must slip something in his morning coffee.

After the workout, our adventures in busing continued. The bus didn't even show. We waited for an hour on a very hot day before we found out it had been sent to pick up players flying into Miami, and we got one of the coaches to shuttle us back in his van.

Things like this happen all the time in the minors, in every organization, and the front office too often doesn't seem concerned. Now, I know there are worse abuses of laborers in the world, and I'd concede that, by and large, athletes are pampered. But it's also true that something like this would never happen in big league camp. There'd be two buses waiting, both air-conditioned, full of sandwiches and refreshments. I can live without the air conditioners (even if they're awesome), and I don't need the sandwiches. It's not the inconvenience that bothers me. It's the indifference.

Thursday, March 15
West Palm Beach

The owner's lockout may be coming to an end. Nothing's been finalized, but rumor has it that opening day might be saved. The younger guys on Montreal's 40-man roster, especially the ones with remote but conceivable chances of making the team out of spring training, must really be sweating it now. They haven't been able to work out at all, of course. A lot of those guys are going to report to big league camp and get sent here before they can even set their bags down. A lot of them, too, are going to get into a few games, and even if they blow the hitters away or bat .500, get sent here. There simply won't be enough time to evaluate the younger players, and more of them than usual are going to be in a tizzy.

In an ordinary year, though, being on the 40-man roster is a big advantage. It sure was for me. The first time I was on a 40-man roster was with San Diego in 1981. I remember receiving the certified letter informing me of my new status. Big deal, I thought. I'd always been invited to big league spring training anyway. Even as ignorant as I was back then, I knew I wasn't going to break camp with the major league club. Being on the 40-man roster meant that I was, without a doubt, a prospect. I took it for granted, though, that I already was a prospect. I was too naive to appreciate the opportunities and privileges that afforded me.

I'd spent the previous year in Double-A, and I showed up in spring training of '81 assuming I'd go to Triple-A. I was mistaken. I *did* go to Triple-A, but I was dead wrong in assuming it. On the last day of spring training, Mark Thurmond and I had a pitch-off. We were to pitch four innings against each other, with the victor going to Hawaii, Triple-A, and the loser going back to Amarillo. There were a couple days of buildup before we squared off. People were placing bets and Triple-A manager Doug Rader called us "his little gladiators." Everybody enjoyed the festivities. Everybody except Mark and me. I asked Eddie Watt—my manager back in Class-A Reno—and Hawaii's pitching coach, Chuck Hartenstein, what would happen if Mark and I had the same results.

"Don't worry," they said. "There *will* be a difference."

The fateful day arrived. Mark allowed one run. So did I. He walked one. Me, too. He allowed three hits. Same with me. He threw fifty-six pitches. Likewise here. "Go sit over there," Doug Rader told us, pointing to a bench. Then the coaching staff, in view but out of earshot, debated our futures. Mark and I didn't say anything.

A few minutes later, Rader broke the news. I went to Triple-A and Mark returned to Amarillo. The decision was based partially on the fact that I was on the 40-man roster and Mark wasn't.

The everyday players joined us today, and it's nice to hear the crack of the bats. I'm also happy to see some other familiar faces, especially some guys who look old enough to vote. Both Randy Braun, a first baseman, and Jose Castro, a third baseman, have played with me before. Jose—we call him Nachi—has been with me in four organizations now. That has to be a current record.

Friday, March 16
West Palm Beach

I threw batting practice today for the first time. I felt strong and pleased with my location.

Montreal seems better at handling pitchers than any organization I've been with. Most teams baby their pitchers for the first week or so, allowing them to throw only fastballs and change-ups. The pitchers actually regress; most of us stay in shape all winter and have been throwing breaking balls for a month or so before spring training begins. Then we're asked to put our sliders and curves on a shelf and, by the time we're allowed to resume spinning them, we've completely lost our release points.

The Expos, though, give each pitcher the responsibility for

taking care of himself. They also like to see us mix up our pitches. Today, they even told me to go after the batters if I felt like it. I've never heard that before in batting practice—much less my first time out.

The hitters are always so far behind the pitchers at this point that it doesn't take much effort to boost my ego during batting practice. But I've been around long enough not to let dominating the hitters during their first week here fatten my ego. They catch up in a hurry.

Saturday, March 17
West Palm Beach

If I spend another year at Triple-A, which I'm sure is all Montreal has in store for me (if that), it'll be my tenth straight year playing at least some of my games at that level. If you'd have told me that in '81, I'd have laughed as hard as any twenty-two-year-old Expos product here would at the same news. But life sneaks up on you.

That first year in Triple-A, I went to Hawaii as the fifth starter and was the ace of the staff by year's end. I went 11–7 and for the first time in my life had a decent breaking ball that I could throw for strikes. I was still basically a thrower with the fastball, though. It's not like I ever had a problem with walks, but I'd be all over the place inside the strike zone. I had no concept of sinking the fastball away from lefties or cutting in on their hands. I'd already lost some velocity from my college days, but I still threw hard enough to get away with being brainless. I was called up to San Diego at the end of the year and had four starts. I pitched well in each game and could have easily gone 4–0. I was 0–1 instead. There wasn't much run support.

This past winter I came home one day and Joey was watching a tape of me pitching against Atlanta in '81. I didn't take his interest too seriously. He was also playing with his G.I. Joe men. I hadn't watched that tape in seven or eight years and I

12

couldn't believe my eyes. I was very unimpressed with what I saw. I threw harder, but the balls were only generally directed toward home plate. My slider hung more often than it bit, and I had absolutely no change-up. All I could do was laugh. I could make a nice living if I could pitch against that guy every fifth day.

When spring training came around in '82, I was ready for it. I thought I had a good chance of making the squad out of camp. That spring proved to be one of the low points in my anonymous career, or at least the turning point in my transition from prospect to suspect.

Every team I've been with has scheduled pitchers the same way during the exhibition season. The starting pitcher is designated for a number of innings, with that number being subject to change, depending upon the amount of pitches thrown.

John Montefusco was listed as the starter on this particular afternoon, with a few others of us to follow. After three or four innings, Dick Williams and pitching coach Norm Sherry (both old-school, my-way-or-the-highway guys) decided John was through for the day. That's fine, except that we were hitting, and there was already one out. Norm came running down into the dugout. Floyd Chiffer and I were the first pitchers he came across. He looked at me. "Can you pitch next inning?"

I assumed he meant in another inning and a half, since it's common practice to be given that much notice in spring training. I assured him I could, but he gathered I didn't sense the urgency of the situation. "No! I mean in the top of the *next* inning!"

This is where it got sticky. I looked at him. "I can't be ready in time for *next* inning," I said.

He looked at Floyd. "Can you?"

Floyd nodded and took off for the pen as the second out was recorded against us. Floyd pitched the following inning and also made the team that spring, although, coming into camp, I had the inside track between the two of us.

The next issue of the *Sporting News* had an account of the

incident, saying something like, "Fireovid Doesn't Want Job." It went on to say how my lack of interest would prevent me from pitching for San Diego and how Floyd had taken a spot away from me. The quotes were from Williams. No reporter ever asked me about it. Why would they, when they got all they needed to know from such a credible source?

Clearly, my response may not have been in the best interest of my career. It *was* honest, though, and I did have my arm's best interest in mind when I said it. I had never been a real reliever, someone who could be pressed into service on short notice. I'd made a couple relief appearances before, but they were always the kind where I was told in the fifth inning that I'd have the eighth. I wasn't telling them I couldn't be a reliever. I was telling them I couldn't be ready to pitch with only a third of an inning to warm up. I would have run the risk of damaging my arm had I tried. Even as a starter, I was notorious for taking a long time to get loose.

Floyd Chiffer, on the other hand, had always been a reliever. Beyond that, he was the type who could get ready with very few pitches. After he was finished that afternoon, he told me how his arm ached and how he was still getting loose as he pitched in the game. That can be (and was) looked upon as having guts. Maybe I was overly protective of my arm and should have approached the circumstances with abandon. Maybe I'd have made the team and secured a future with the Padres.

And maybe I'd have blown my arm out.

I think Sherry lost sight of how many pitches were thrown and figured out that Montefusco was done only seconds before he ran into the dugout. Sherry messed up and he panicked. He came to me first because I was the first pitcher in his path, and Floyd was then asked only because I'd said no. He had a second to see that "yes" was the right answer.

It's not as though a Cy Young Award winner's career was cut short by what happened. Williams and Sherry may not even remember the day. And even if they did, they could easily deny or support whatever they wished. They could say it was a pre-determined test to see how I'd respond, or something like that.

Let me tie this up with two questions.

Consider the impact this had on each person involved. Who do you feel would tend to recall it best? Also, if they were to dismiss my account as nonsense, couldn't I dismiss the conclusion they drew at the time, that I somehow didn't want a big league job, as even bigger nonsense?

This afternoon, Rick Williams, Montreal's head minor league pitching instructor, called me aside. Rick's about my age, and, until he blew his arm out a few years back, he'd been a left-handed pitching prospect in the Expos organization. He blew his arm out so bad, in fact, that he simply doesn't throw anymore. He uses a fungo bat, and he's more accurate with that than most guys are with their arms.

He's also Dick Williams's son.

Happily, other than having a mustache, he doesn't seem to be anything like his father. Rick's an up-front, personable, hyperkinetic guy, the sort of person who runs from field to field inspecting his troops. He wanted to know my thoughts coming into camp, particularly if I viewed myself exclusively as a starter.

"That's what I'm best suited for," I said.

He nodded. He just seemed to be familiarizing himself with people new to the Expos. "Listen," he said. "I'd appreciate any input you could give me on how camp's being run."

I just looked at him. "You bet," I said. "I appreciate you asking." It's hard to imagine Dick Williams's genes in this man.

Sunday, March 18
West Palm Beach

We hear rumors about the lockout every few hours, and each new rumor seems to contradict the one before it. But the rumor we heard today caused a lot of excitement at minor league camp. The owners' new offer supposedly would allow each team to carry thirty players for the first month of the season. The rules allow twenty-five, although teams have informally agreed the past few years to carry only twenty-four. Thirty, though, would probably mean that teams would carry four or five extra pitchers, since our arms wouldn't be strong enough yet to last very long into games.

Even a temporary roster expansion like this could be a big deal. Anything can happen in a month's exposure. It's a chance to prove you belong. Established big leaguers and bonus babies have to prove they *don't* belong. The rest of us have to prove that we *do*.

I could swear I borrowed someone else's windup this morning. I released the ball from every possible arm slot—a couple times, too, from impossible slots. At the end of my delivery, my left foot landed all over the place. Throwing strikes isn't typically a problem for me; last season, I averaged only one walk per six innings pitched. Even if I'm unable to locate the ball where I want it, I can at least get it over the plate. Today I struggled to do that. During the course of my performance today, I started out trying to hit the corners and finished up hoping only that I'd get the ball somewhere inside the batting cage without hurting anybody.

Tomorrow we start games. The day after that, I get an inning.

My boys called tonight. Joey's about to lose a front tooth. I know there'll be more eventful moments in his life, but it hurts to be separated at times when he's so fired up. So many people seem to envy the traveling that professional athletes do. When I retire from this game, I'm definitely finding some nine-to-five job. I've traveled enough. I've missed more than enough.

Monday, March 19
West Palm Beach

The lockout's over. The players signed an agreement late last night. We still don't know all the details, but about ten pitchers here will be leaving for major league camp. I'm staying here. And I'd be lying if I said I wasn't bitter.

Last year I tied for the league lead in wins and threw a complete-game victory over Indianapolis, Montreal's Triple-A team, in the playoffs. I look at the guys going to big league camp and it wounds my pride. I *know* I've got as much to offer as most of them. My age is no longer a plus, but other guys my age— and older—are going. Joaquin Andujar is going. He showed up here a couple days ago. He doesn't run with us or do any of the drills. He pitched this past winter in the senior League. He didn't pitch at all last season. He's thirty-seven. And he's supposedly getting a shot to make the Expos' rotation.

Over the years, I've learned to channel bitterness into motivation. It's not a spontaneous process, though.

And there is one small positive to all this: my roommate left for big league camp and the team's going to let me have my own room for the rest of spring training.

I know I can't sit on the pity pot for long. If I dwelled on every negative, I'd have been out of this game a long time ago. Not because I'd have quit, either. My negativism would have shown up in my performance, sooner or later, and I'd have been asked to leave. My chances are slim, but if I weren't in uniform, they'd be none.

Tuesday, March 20
West Palm Beach

Today we played Atlanta's Triple-A squad. We won, 5—1, and I had a three-up, three-down inning. The first time out against real opposition is always a little goofy. Managers and pitching coaches stress how trivial the first outing is. "Just throw strikes," they'll say. But to any pitcher whose roster spot isn't cast in stone—and there aren't many whose are—each appearance is important. Decisions in this game don't make themselves. Obviously, a kid isn't going to jump from rookie ball to Double-A just because he tossed two scoreless innings in March. But even though final rosters are still a ways off, players are already jockeying for position.

Most decisions are—and should be—made over the winter, based largely upon a player's progress the previous season. In spring training, it's then the player's responsibility either to solidify advances he's already made or to perform so well that management has to reevaluate its preconceived notions. Or both. Occasionally, though, a job is wide open and goes to the player who has the best spring. Players are told this all the time, of course. Once in a while, it's the truth.

All I can do is throw well. After that, it's out of my hands. I recorded three outs on three different pitches today. I threw eight strikes and three balls. I got batters to hit two weak grounders and a pop-up to second. I walked no one. Most pitchers will tell you immediately how many they struck out—or "blew away." When you blow away as few batters as I do, you adapt your report card to accentuate other positives. I walked no one.

Wednesday, March 21
West Palm Beach

Because of the length of the lockout, opening day in the major leagues has been pushed back a week. That means instead of the normal six weeks to prepare, clubs are left with three. With that in mind, Montreal has decided it doesn't have enough time to look at all its prospects. Today was the first official day of big league spring training, and they've already sent down five players to us. Also, the ten pitchers who left here for major league camp has been reduced to four, for the same reason. I'd imagine most organizations are following suit. I won't feel so isolated after all.

Keith Atherton retired today. He'd said when he came here that he'd either break camp with Montreal or quit. His arm had been bothering him, and it was obvious he wasn't going to leave Florida on the major league roster. He talked with Rick Williams this morning while we were shagging. Then he just left. Only a few guys knew what was going on. I didn't even notice he'd gone. I've pitched against Keith several times and gotten to know him a little bit this spring. Most experienced players, me included, are calloused to the arrivals and departures of others. Over a summer's time, I'll develop two or three friendships that are extremely close and brutally honest, and then often I'll never see or hear from those people again. I've had twenty or thirty friendships that will never be matched once I'm out of the game. I couldn't tell you where half of them live now.

Tomorrow we're on the road to play the Mets. I'm scheduled to go three innings, which is a good sign. I've been in enough spring trainings to know they don't waste extended innings on pitchers who aren't in their plans. Plus I was shown a list not yet posted that had me going four innings five days later. It's my job to verify what appears to be their intentions. It'd be flat-out stupid to assume anything right now.

Thursday, March 22
West Palm Beach

We had a blowout today. We beat New York 18–1. I completed my three innings as planned. I only threw thirty-six pitches, twenty-six of them strikes. I didn't walk anybody, and I did manage a strikeout. I fanned the very first man I faced and immediately thought I might get a few. Realistically, I should have known I'd hit my quota for the day. There was only one real ugly pitch. I hung a slider to their cleanup hitter, Kelvin Torve, and he jumped all over it. Evidently he figured pulling it out to left would have been too easy, so he tried parking it to straightaway center. He must feel humbled, because he only short-hopped the wall out there. I gave up three hits all together and for the most part had a decent idea where I was putting

19

it, as well as how much I was putting behind it. The shoulder again felt fine.

It was a fun game to watch, at least from our bench. Everyone who's been in baseball for any length of time has witnessed this type of game. I've played in games like that before from the other end, and it's no fun. There is some luck in baseball and today we had all of it, although nearly all of our twenty-seven hits were scalded. Our manager, Tim Johnson, didn't even make the players do their usual postgame running; they'd been circling the bases all afternoon.

For my part, I'm glad for all the runs they scored for me today. I'm doubly glad I don't pitch tomorrow. There are two days most pitchers like to stay away from. One is the day your team's bat order comes in. The guys tear open those boxes, just like Christmas morning. They count the grains of each bat, they shave the handles down and—once the game starts —they swing their new toys at any pitch that comes within an area code of the strike zone.

The other day to avoid is the day after you've crushed somebody. Things have a way of evening out. A team that's just given up eighteen runs has a lot of evening out to do.

Friday, March 23
West Palm Beach

Today stunk. Yesterday was a scorcher, and I worked up a healthy lather. At minor league camp we get our uniforms washed every other day. Yesterday wasn't my turn. Today I had a jersey that served as a reminder. Funk followed me everywhere I went on the field this morning. There are around 140–150 players here and two or three washers and driers to serve them. We do get all of our personal garments cleaned daily, so it's not gross where sanitation is concerned. It's simply impossible for the clubhouse people to run every player's uniform through every day. Most teams do this, too, not just Montreal. There's no way around it unless I'd bring my uniform home and wash it at the hotel. I'm here to make a team, though, not a fashion statement. Besides, I don't believe I'm the only one here who sweats.

My arm rebounded so well from yesterday it's scary. For years now, I've expected my shoulder to bark the day after, and it's always obliged. When I began to toss today, I realized right away something was different. Better. Thirty-six pitches isn't a complete game, but I'm familiar enough with my shoulder to know it's usually enough to hurt. I started throwing harder today to bring it about and felt nothing. Tomorrow I'm supposed to do some work on the side, so it'll all come out in the wash, just like my uniform.

Saturday, March 24
West Palm Beach

I had a brief morning at the yard today, as did most pitchers. I was dressed at 9:00 and finished at 10:30. I had a most productive day, though. I stretched, had a workout on the side for fifteen minutes, ran for twenty-five minutes, and did my weights. The Expos aren't big on having pitchers shag fly balls for hours on end, so we ordinarily don't graze in the outfield during batting practice. The pitchers appreciate it, plus we know (or hope) we'll get our share of it once the season starts.

Rick Williams worked with me some today from the stretch. I've always had a slow leg kick, and I'm trying to abandon it. It's awkward right now, because if I'm too quick to the plate my arm doesn't have enough time to catch up with the rest of my body and I throw nothing but pus. There's no problem in taking some time off my delivery, but I can't sacrifice location or velocity in the process.

Rick also told me I'm pitching four innings this coming Tuesday and again five days later, April 1, probably for five innings. I'm no math major but I can see my innings are increasing. I can also add five to one. Opening day for Indianapolis is April 6. Right now, it looks like I might be opening-day pitcher. On the other hand, I might be sent home a week from now, too.

One thing is for sure. It's all happening fast. Opening day is in less than two weeks, whether I'm there or not. I really haven't had much experience in minor league camp throughout my career. Except for this spring, it's a couple weeks shorter than major league camp, and that makes a ton of difference. Guys are already talking about the upcoming season, but it seems like I just got here, baseballwise.

Funny, though; I talk to Patty or the boys, and it seems like I've been here forever.

Sunday, March 25
West Palm Beach

There are still seventeen or eighteen pitchers at big league camp. Because of the lockout, clubs will most likely carry eleven or twelve pitchers for a few weeks, allowed to prevent injuries. That means Montreal still has to send quite a few people down—or else release them, which is always a possibility. Whatever happens, one predicament becomes increasingly apparent. There are far too many bodies for available jobs. We're rapidly closing in on that period of spring training which lays to rest hundreds of grown men's baseball careers.

When I was younger and a friend was released, it seemed like a tragedy. Four or five of us would take the guy out, determined to give him a night he'd never forget, although we'd drink enough beer to produce quite the opposite result. We'd all tell him how he'd been screwed, even if deep down we knew he never really had the tools. For years, I took it to heart much more than I should have. I was so naive about how the system works, how it *has* to work.

Dale Mohorcic is a good friend of mine here in camp. I pitched against Horse back in rookie ball, when he was in

Victoria and I was in Walla Walla (there really is such a place; I liked it, too). We've also played together in Puerto Rico. Both of our careers have been roller coasters, although his ride has peaked at a higher elevation. If I showed up at the park to-morrow and was given my release, Horse is one person I'd say so long to. After breaking my hand shaking it, Horse would ask me what I was going to do and wish me well. The second I left, he'd never give it a second thought and bear down to avoid the same fortune. I'd be the same way if he was released. It's not cold; we just understand the game and our place in it. It's a rude awakening though, for some twenty-year-old, who wouldn't have that sense of perspective, to be told he'll never fulfill his childhood dreams. And it's going to start happening.

Monday, March 26
West Palm Beach

Sure enough, Rick Williams took several individuals aside to-day for private conversations. To my knowledge, nobody was axed. They were, however, warned about all the arms we have in camp here and, by implication, braced for what that logjam might mean. These guys may not necessarily be going home, but they may not be destined for the level of ball they'd antic-ipated, either. That's not as devastating as a release, but it can be degrading. Most times, these kids are a couple years out of high school or college, where they were all-conference, all-state, or all-world, and teams were built around their dominant abil-ity. They're being told "no" for the first time, and, in many cases, insecurity surfaces, also for the first time. It's not an uplifting experience no matter who you are. Lots of guys here are gearing themselves for Triple-A and will be assigned to A ball, not even Double-A.

Rick called me over this morning, too. He asked if I'd ever considered coaching after I was finished as a player. At least he didn't tell me I was *already* through. I've had coaching offers before, and I was particularly honored by this one, since I respect Montreal's approach so much. But I told Rick I couldn't really think about coaching now. I have to think about playing.

I saw in the paper today that Keith Atherton rejoined the Minnesota Twins and was invited to major league camp. Evidently he wasn't ready to retire after all. All he needed was another chance. I've thought about quitting many times in the past several years. I'd have a family to go home to, and I could leave this futility. Patty and the boys still support me, although at times I think they're the only ones who still believe in me. There's futility in all walks of life, I guess. I'm lucky to enjoy the job I'm fighting to keep.

Tuesday, March 27
West Palm Beach

I went four innings this afternoon, as planned. Just because I'm scheduled for four doesn't mean I'll last four, even if I'm not giving up runs. There's a pitch limit enforced on every outing. It's a pretty safe bet, though, that if a pitcher is closing in on his limit, he's getting roughed up. Anyway, I walked one, struck out one, and gave up three hits. Unfortunately, one of those hits was a blast. I was tinkering with my mechanics and wasn't as focused on location as I needed to be. It was a hideous pitch, and the batter disposed of it accordingly.

My arm felt super, but the rest of my body must still think the lockout's in effect. My lower back aches, the left half of my bottom hurts from landing, and, since I've gotten back to the hotel, my legs have cramped a couple times. I know dehydration caused the spasms, but beyond that I suspect age is the culprit. When I got in the clubhouse and sat down in front of my locker, I felt like I needed a spatula to get up. After a few more times out, the body will adjust to the abuse, and it shouldn't react this way. It shouldn't. That doesn't mean it won't. Every year it's more difficult. I should add that I'm in great shape, too. A pitcher can't train his body for what it expends in game situations.

Seven or eight players were released yesterday, and I heard that more were today. I hadn't even noticed, so they must have all been at lower levels. There are so many bodies here that no one would take note unless he knew the guy.

Again, it's perspective. It's comfortable for players like me who've been kicked around to complain and recall how we've been wronged in our careers. Sometimes we need to stop and realize that at least we've *had* our careers.

Wednesday, March 28
West Palm Beach

I went to the park early this morning to do some extra work on my shoulder. Since my arm's been healthy, I haven't had much reason to go into the training room this spring. It's a zoo in there. There are three tables and three trainers to serve everybody here. Two trainers quit last week due to the additional work required of them.

I don't blame them. These guys have to help with laundry, hang up uniforms, and do all sorts of general maintenance in the clubhouse. The Indianapolis trainer, John Spinosa, was telling me today how the younger players take so much of his time. They don't know what they need or want and can't be trusted to help themselves to any minor medication. Many— too many—of these kids even go to John to have him apply Band-Aids to their ouchies. What's worse, he said, is that in many cases they're without a father or mother figure for the first time. The closest person in baseball to filling that void is the trainer. Like most minor league trainers, John seems to be kind of an irritable guy. Minor league trainers have a lot to be irritated about.

It's not the same in major league camp. Trainers have state-of-the-art facilities. Players aren't wondering if the tables they lie on were once occupied by Babe Ruth. At first, there's only fifty to sixty players to deal with—and then, by the end of spring training, just twenty-five.

I don't believe there were any more releases today. Players are now being moved from one level to the next. No one is moving up.

Thursday, March 29
West Palm Beach

The owners announced last night that they've dropped their original plan of carrying twenty-seven players until May 1. Major league rosters will include twenty-five as usual, in spite of time lost over the lockout. We all learned about the decision this morning. It'll have a definite impact on moves made all through the organization, especially with pitchers. Eventually, most guys will get sent to the level they'd have gone to had there not been a lockout. But this does force management to construct all the teams earlier than planned. The domino effect would have filtered down the ranks, anyway, as players were reassigned at the close of April. Now it'll happen sooner.

This is an uneasy time of year for everybody. All over the various spring trainings, hundreds of men are entering their respective clubhouses sheepishly, waiting for a note or a nudge to see the farm director. We players often overlook the uneasiness these determinations (or terminations) cause coaching staffs. Rick Williams has told me a couple of times how he hates this time period and John Boles, who is the field coordinator here, has said the same. It can't possibly be a pleasure to tell anyone he's finished.

I worked today on a new change-up. It went well, and I have to use it. I've been a fastball/slider pitcher my entire career. I've had a change-up, but it's never been consistent, so I rarely used it. I'm going to use it this season; without it, I'll never

26

get back to the big leagues. My fastball isn't as fast as it used to be and my slider doesn't fall off the table.

However, I have one thing I never took to the mound years ago: a brain.

Friday, March 30
West Palm Beach

I heard through the grapevine that there were a number of releases again this morning. Opening day for Indianapolis is a week from today and the Double-A team, Jacksonville, opens even earlier. Innings now are issued only to those in good standing. I heard one pitcher in our group, a righthander named Jim Jefferson, expressing some confusion because he'd been scheduled to throw today and then, this morning, discovered his name wasn't on the list anymore. He should have known that this apparent oversight was no accident. No one had the heart to tell him. Maybe ignorance is bliss after all.

John Spinosa asked me today what number I wanted on my jersey this season. That's a *great* omen. My boys are big Joe Montana fans, and they want me to wear 16, which is hardly a pitcher's number. Actually, most players are selective when it comes to their numbers. Scott Anderson told me I "looked" more like a 16 than a 22. Actually I "feel" like a 47. What's important is that I was asked. That was no accident either.

I've been working my butt off here. In addition to what's required, I do weights a lot, and—every day in my hotel room—I do a hundred sit-ups and seventy push-ups. I'm also avoiding the beer and watching what I eat.

When I think about all the times I felt I was deserving and didn't get the call, I have to think of something else, as quickly as I can. Those thoughts are like a cancer. I'd be lying if I said it didn't bother me. If this is my final year, I'm not going to leave it to chance. I'll retire knowing I did everything I could.

Of course, I'd really rather not retire at all.

Saturday, March 31
West Palm Beach

Joe Kerrigan, the Indianapolis pitching coach, told me that I'll start the second game of the year. I couldn't care less which game it is, just so I'm in the rotation somewhere. We open in Des Moines against the Cubs for three games and then travel to Omaha for another three. The way it's set up now, I'd get the Cubs, skip Omaha, and then meet the Cubs again in our home opener. Whatever happens, I'm relieved to know I'll be starting.

The Indianapolis Indians have won the league championship and playoffs the last four years. I've never been associated with a team at any level that's had a rich winning tradition. I haven't been on a team that's won it all since high school, and that was fifteen years ago. In the last couple years I developed a hatred for the Indianapolis team. Some of it was jealousy, although some, too, was deserved. A couple of their players, guys who are no longer here, were arrogant showboats. Everybody hated the Indians. (Notice the past tense already. The season hasn't even begun and it feels so different to be one of "those" guys.) Hating Indianapolis was the Triple-A equivalent of hating the Yankees.

The next news I want to hear is who else is in the Indianapolis rotation and who's in the Montreal rotation. I need to get a feel for what's going on and where I stand. This won't affect how *I* throw, but, in my career, I've learned to recognize prospects, suspects, and no-respects. It would be an easier game to understand if statistics dictated moves. It rarely works that way, though. An honest manager, pitching coach, or minor league director would tell you the same. If I have the ball in my hand every five days and stink up the place, I don't have a leg to stand on. But I can also pitch well, and go nowhere.

It's not the same for the blue-chip prospects, although even they don't have any guarantees. I know. I was one of those guys once.

April

Sunday, April 1
West Palm Beach

I went five innings today. It was the final tune-up in a game situation before the season starts, and I didn't really want to close down here with a poor showing. I did pitch well, allowing no runs, three hits, no walks, striking out four. I got two outs with the change-up and threw an acceptable percentage of strikes with it. They hit a lot of ground balls, which is the best barometer of my stuff.

I also got to the plate twice. Both times called for a bunt, though, so I was saved the embarrassment of swinging away. I moved the runners over both times, and they wound up scoring. I wasn't giving everybody high fives, but I felt a little responsible for the runs. The ball comes in there in a hurry. I haven't hit since '84, and I'd forgotten how hard grown men can throw a baseball. I can pretty much dominate my boys in Wiffle ball, and the pitching machines we use just aren't the same as live arms. Machines don't generate as much velocity and they're more predictable with location. In other words, machines don't provide the element of fear. I felt more like a participant than I have with American League clubs.

31

The rotation has been modified again. I'll have the first game in Des Moines after all. This, of course, is subject to change.

After careful deliberation with the family, I'll wear number 16. My five-year-old, Sammy, says that now I can pretend I'm Joe Montana. And to think: all these years I've thought my boys idolized *me*.

Monday, April 2
West Palm Beach

There were massive amounts of releases this morning, along with several demotions. As soon as I walked into the clubhouse, I could sense a more formal atmosphere. The volume was down from the normal chaos. I passed Scott Anderson sitting at his locker and asked him what was going on. As if I didn't know. "There's a lot of guys walking out of here," he said, "with their bags over their shoulders."

I made it over to my locker and just sat and watched. Before I was warm in my seat the coaches had summoned three players to the back room. It's a bad feeling and I can sympathize, but life goes on, and I have goals of my own. Still, it's tough to watch the tears.

James Steels has goals, too. I played with James way back when we were Padres. He has a quick bat with some pop from the left side. Yesterday he was called over to play in the major league game. Usually people from minor league camp never play in these games. They're just there in case a stud gets hurt. James, an experienced player, wasn't overly excited about the invitation but was willing, if not exactly happy, to oblige. James aired his gripe, though, to Tom Runnels, James's manager in Indy last year and now the Montreal third-base coach. "You're familiar with me, or should be," James said. "You know what I can do. You didn't care for me enough to invite me to big league camp. So don't ask me over to watch your boys play and expect me to be all smiles."

A twenty-one-year-old might not feel this way and wouldn't

be wise to express it if he did. James has been around the block a couple times, though.

It got worse. When James arrived at the park and started taking batting practice, Hal McRae, the Expos' major league hitting instructor, greeted him as "Walter." That'd be the equivalent of the major league pitching coach, Larry Bearnarth, not knowing my name—which is a possibility, come to think of it, since we've never met. But James is no stranger to this organization. I guess now he has a better idea of where he stands in the corporate ladder, and a new nickname as well. We joke about it, but it has to hurt James some. He's working as hard as any of the millionaires, and he's an unknown, literally. Walter Steels. That stinks.

Tuesday, April 3
West Palm Beach

Today, we all had a brief stay at the yard. We were dressed at nine and started an intrasquad game against the Double-A team at ten. They broke camp later in the day for Jacksonville, where they'll begin the season. We have two days before we leave for Des Moines. We survivors have cabin fever.

The major league owners have retracted their refusal for expanded rosters through April. Once again, there will be twenty-seven players allowed. People here don't care much about it now. If you're established it won't affect you, and if you're in limbo, worrying won't do you any good.

Wednesday, April 4
West Palm Beach

This is the last full day down here. Tomorrow we have an early workout and head for the airport at 11 A.M. Everybody said their good-byes and good lucks today. Unfortunately, the coaching staff had a few good-byes of their own, too. Jim Jefferson was released. He hadn't thrown much, but whenever I saw him he pitched well. He'd been working with the Indy group all spring. We asked him the standard questions. "Where you gonna go? What you gonna do? Do you have a job to fall back on? What about your family?" There's a lot more Jim Jeffersons going home this spring than superstars gearing for the season.

I stopped in to thank John Boles this morning. If it weren't for John, I'd be entering my fourth year of retirement from this game. I have my complaints about things that haven't gone my way in baseball, and, from time to time, I have brief bouts with resentment. But I also have to be thankful for John. Without him all these fierce and wonderful emotions wouldn't be possible.

Thursday, April 5
Des Moines

We arrived in Des Moines early this evening. It's supposed to get down into the teens tonight and the forecast is the same for tomorrow. I used to like throwing in cold weather, but it's no fun at all anymore. When my shoulder gets in certain positions I feel a little pain. Still, it feels much better than the past two years.

I talked with Angel Morris before I left Florida. Angel is a catcher who came over in a trade from the Royals last winter. He played Double-A last year with Kansas City. He played winter ball in Puerto Rico, arguably the most competitive winter league, and finished sixth in batting. He was 7-for-16 during spring training. He had been with the Triple-A team all spring. Yesterday he was told he'd play in the Florida State League for an independent team until there's room for him elsewhere.

He's screwed. First of all, the Florida State League is Class-A ball. Angel has no business going there. Secondly, indepen-

dent teams are basically for leftover players from various organizations. There's no solid affiliation with the parent club,
which means Angel's performance won't be monitored as
closely as others'. Finally, we have four catchers on our team
now. When is there going to be room for him here? I would bet
our catching situation will be thinned out shortly. We certainly
don't need another. Hopefully something will materialize in
Double-A for him.

"At least I'm still getting paid," Angel told me. Baseball is
his job. He isn't going to buy a third home with this month's
pay. He needs baseball to support his family for the spring and
summer months. I'm sure his dreams are as vivid as those of
any player in the major leagues. His is just more of a blue-collar
work ethic.

Friday, April 6
Des Moines

We started off the season on the right foot. We won 4–2. The
temperature never dipped as low as projected, but 30 degrees
is still plenty cold for baseball, especially when the wind picked
up. I pitched all right. I went 5⅓ innings and gave up the two
runs. We were behind when I came out, so I didn't get the win.
I could have earned a loss, though, and didn't. I wasn't sharp
and labored most of the game. I walked two and managed to
strike out their pitcher once. It's an okay outing, given the
weather.

Personally, I thought the umpire's strike zone was a little
tight, too.

Baseball's a funny game. Our third baseman is Jose Castro.
He struck out his first three times up, and looked foolish doing
it. He couldn't have hit the ball with an oar. The fourth time,
he came up with the bases drunk and lined the first pitch to
left-center, driving in all three men. He went from goat to hero
in one pitch.

Opening day in Des Moines isn't quite the same as it is in Cincinnati, the traditional major league opener. After I completed my warm-up pitches for the fourth inning, the umpire motioned for time out and pointed to center field. I turned around and waited for a couple minutes while one of the grounds-crew guys struggled to hoist the flag. After getting it to half-mast, he gave up, got on his tractor, and drove off the field. I thought that was where the flag was supposed to be— like maybe someone in Iowa had died or something—until the game was delayed again the next half-inning while he finally went back out and raised it to the top.

Saturday, April 7
Des Moines

We had our lunch handed to us tonight, 16–2. None of our pitchers escaped unscathed. Howard Farmer started for us. In four innings, he gave up ten hits, two walks, and seven runs. Howard, though, is one of Montreal's boys. By that I mean he's a highly touted, reed-thin, twenty-four-year-old prospect with a "can't miss" label. Despite his outing tonight, he deserves all the attention the Expos give him. Less than a week ago he shut out the Mets for five innings while still in big league camp. He has three attributes that, combined, make all the brass salivate. He has a live arm. He ordinarily has great command of three pitches. And he's young.

We walked back to the hotel together after the game was finished. He seemed composed about his effort, but he had already had five innings in the clubhouse to absorb it. He didn't complain too much, didn't offer a lot of excuses, and, finally, laughed about what had happened. If indeed he was shell-shocked, he masked it well. Often, a young talent will take hitters lightly when he reads and hears how dominating he's supposed to be. I don't know if that's what took place with Howard tonight or not. I do know that, now, the Iowa Cubs have his respect.

A black cat ran across the field tonight in the seventh inning. You see this kind of stuff in the minors from time to time, and it's a reminder of where I am. Animals have a tougher time gaining access to major league stadiums.

Sunday, April 8
Des Moines

I shagged fly balls with Chris Marchok during batting practice today. There are several differences between us. He's a reliever; I'm a starter. He's lefthanded; I'm right. He's young; I'm not. He's spending his first season at Triple-A; I'm spending my tenth. He's an idealist. I'm a realist. He's single. I'm married. He graduated from Harvard. I didn't. We're both blond.

Unfortunately, he got his feet wet in Triple-A by appearing in the massacre last night. He was our most effective pitcher in that game, even though he gave up two runs in two innings. He said he'd been a little anxious because it was his first outing and hoped he'd be more comfortable next time. He was. Today he tossed two scoreless frames and earned the win.

The real star of our 9–5 win today was Jerry Goff, who had eight runs batted in. That may be the most I've ever seen. James Steels had a distinction also. In the fifth inning, he drifted back from his center-field position to snare a fly ball and caught his spikes under the wall. The game had to be stopped while the grounds crew helped him escape. He's lucky he didn't wreck his ankle.

We rode the two hours to Omaha after the game, in a bus so tiny we had to put all our baseball gear in the aisles. Nobody complained. We all remember being in the lower minors, packed into smaller buses than this and on the road for fifteen-hour stretches. Except on short trips like today's, we fly everywhere here.

Still, all baseball buses are sort of the same. The farther you venture from the front, the noisier it gets. Headphones are as necessary in pro baseball as jockstraps.

Monday, April 9
Omaha

We lost a heartbreaker tonight, 2–1. My roommate, Scott Anderson—a deep-voiced, bony, six-six Oregonian—pitched an outstanding game. He went 7⅔ innings and was charged with one run. He left the game ahead 1–0 with a runner on first. Chris Marchok came in and had their cleanup hitter struck out, but the umpire either went temporarily blind or lacked the guts to ring the guy up. The hitter wound up with a walk. The next man up squeaked a ground ball through the infield to tie the game.

There's so much more at stake in minor league games than the team winning or losing. Scott is twenty-seven years old, and although he's far from being over the hill, he's at an age where he needs strong stats to get back to the major leagues. Generally, the older a player is, the more convincing he has to be. The front office is hesitant to trust decent numbers from an older player. If he's *that* good, they reason, why wasn't he up years ago? When Scott throws like he did tonight, he needs to get the win. Clubs are waiting to give opportunities to the Howard Farmers. Scott Anderson, and the rest of us Scott Andersons, have to *make* our opportunities. I'm realistic about, not bitter toward, the Howard Farmers. To be honest, I'd evaluate talent the same way if I were a general manager.

Scott will have twenty-some more starts this season, and if he matches tonight's display every time, he'll get the call. Obviously, he won't do it; no one's that good every night.

Tuesday, April 10
Omaha

Tonight's game has been postponed due to cold weather. It's expected to get down in the teens, with snow flurries and gusting winds thrown in for good measure. We've all played in worse so it kind of caught us off guard. Omaha has announced a doubleheader for tomorrow and I've been informed I'll pitch the first game.

Minor league players relish cancellations in any form because there are so few off days scheduled during the season, many fewer than in the big leagues. Tonight's night off isn't as appreciated as one would be in August, when we've played in the heat every day for a month. I really do know of guys who have, like the scene in *Bull Durham*, snuck into their park at night and flooded the field to assure a break in the action.

The question now is what I'm going to do for the evening. I've been invited to go to a movie, go to a mall, play poker, or, most recently, to go out and get "shit-faced." Every day—every night, too—there's so much time to kill. Still, I turned all my invites down, politely. I lay on the bed and watched CNN, listening as most of the guys headed to see the bright lights of Omaha. The motel got quieter and quieter. Most motels have a little table near the window, lit by some hanging lamp, and I sat at mine, in my underwear, writing letters on the complimentary motel stationery.

Then I made a few phone calls, trying to line up an apartment in Indianapolis. Once I settled that, I called to arrange for some furniture to rent. My pad will be the reference-standard generic apartment. Then I called to have cable hooked up.

Patty will bring me some pots, pans, silverware, clothes, drapes, a shower curtain—and whatever else she remembers. After all the times I've uprooted her, she has moving down to an art. She's also had babies Joey and Sammy to accompany her everywhere. Now that they're school-aged—first grade and preschool—she can only bring them for occasional visits.

People tell her all the time what an exciting and romantic life she must lead as a baseball wife. Usually, she has the self-discipline to bite her tongue and flash a polite smile. Sometimes, though, she gives them an earful.

Wednesday, April 11
Omaha

If this weather keeps up, they're going to have to change the name of the league to the Alaskan Association. I pitched the first game in what the weathermen like to call gale-force winds. I didn't even want to *know* the temperature. During the game, most of the team stayed in the clubhouse.

We got beat 3–1. I pitched five innings and surrendered all three runs. I uncharacteristically walked three and fanned three. I struck out the side in the second inning. I haven't done that in a decade—no joke. In the third, my body was out in front of my arm, and I wasn't able to correct it until after the inning was completed. My strengths, normally, are throwing strikes and making adjustments out on the mound. Tonight I could do neither.

The second game was canceled—too late to save me, but the other guys were happy.

We're all eager to get to Indy tomorrow. It'll be great to see the family again. Patty's coming as soon as Joey gets out of school. Bryan is only three hours from Indy, as close as to any other place I've played. The boys tell me on the phone that they're fired up to see me, and I tell them I'm fired up to see them, and we get into a debate about who's the most fired up. Patty rules it a tie.

Sammy doesn't know it yet, but I got him a new glove. I have a contract with Rawlings and am entitled to two gloves a year. I've been wearing it whenever possible to soften it up some for him. Joey's found that the best way to keep his soft is to leave it out in the rain. There aren't too many five- and seven-year-olds running around with hundred-dollar infielders' gloves.

Thursday, April 12
Indianapolis

We have a rare day off today, sort of. Currently, I'm above the clouds somewhere between Omaha and Chicago. Our flights are almost always at the crack of dawn. Scott and I have been up since 5 A.M.

Like everything else, it's different in the big leagues. Teams often use chartered flights to transport the squad. The players are bused to the airport following that evening's game, boarded onto their plane, and flown directly to the next city. If they sit in middle seats, it's because of stupidity, not necessity. Upon arrival, two buses are waiting and they're taken to their hotel. The luggage is delivered to the hotel later and bellboys happily distribute the belongings. The following day may very well be an off day or "travel day," too. I shouldn't complain. Talk to a kid in the Texas League about the dusty bus ride from El Paso to Jackson.

The reason this isn't a complete day off is that we have a banquet to attend tonight. These are the same in every minor league town. Players are always told to mingle with the crowd. More than likely, I'll sit at a table with some affluent, well-meaning people and try to answer questions politely with my mouth full. I guarantee I'll hear about their great uncle's second son (or was it his third?), who was a heck of a ballplayer and went to a tryout camp once. The kid got screwed over or injured, and I'm supposed to shake my head and feel pity for him because now he's gone on to become a doctor or lawyer and gets to spend every night with his family. Poor guy. The worst question I get, though, and I always get it, is whether I think I'll ever make it to the "pros."

Our flight was delayed four hours in Chicago. Now I have just enough time to shower, change clothes, and head for the festivities. Patty and the boys were going to try to get here in time to accompany me, but they didn't make it. Patty is a blue-jeans-and-sweatshirt girl, so she isn't drawn to these events either. We haven't seen each other in five weeks, though, and we would really like to be together, no matter what the circumstances.

Friday, April 13
Indianapolis

We won our home opener 6–2 tonight, and, even though it rained the entire game, Bush Stadium was nearly full. Scott and I could relate to the fans, since we were in street clothes up in the stands with them. Scott was operating the camera and I had the radar gun. In the minor leagues, starting pitchers often have duties on days they're not throwing. I'll be in the stands for forty percent of our games this year, as I was the last two years with the Royals. After a while, you don't even feel like part of the team.

There was a major screwup today. We wear our white uniforms at home and our owner, Max Schumaker, was gracious enough to purchase new pants this year. In the big leagues, players are measured during spring training to insure a comfortable, stylish fit. Players can also request the length of their pants, sort of an individual trademark to wearing a uniform. There aren't, of course, any measurements taken here, and the length of the pants are all the same, give or take an inch. Wild Bill Neely, our clubhouse attendant, handed out the pants. Wild Bill's a stocky, volatile, fortyish man who spends the better part of his days asleep on the trainer's table, and none of us hesitated letting him know what we thought of our pants. Jim Davins, one of our relievers, received the worst pants of us all. He was afraid the wind might pick up and blow him away. His legs looked like masts surrounded by sails. He just laughed it off.

Jose Castro wasn't laughing, though. This is the fourth different organization I've played with Jose so I've learned to read him over the years. He just walked around and kept saying, to

42

nobody in particular, "How can *anyone* wear these things? *I* can't wear these things." His attitude was really messed up as a result of it. He not only wanted new pants, he wanted the head of whoever was responsible. Failing that, he just about settled for Wild Bill's.

Jose will feel better tomorrow, though. He took his pants to be altered.

Saturday, April 14
Indianapolis

I was up in the stands again tonight videotaping every pitch we threw. Each pitcher has his own cassette to refer to. Joe Kerrigan will study all the deliveries and determine if any slight adjustments should be experimented with to improve location or velocity. I'm sure he'll view Travis Chambers very closely tomorrow morning. We were ahead 5–3 entering the ninth inning tonight, and lost 7–5. Travis is our short man, and it's his job to protect leads late in the game. Everything fell apart for him in the ninth. We all felt dejected afterward, but nobody more than Travis.

I've relieved some in my career and it's an awful lonely feeling to lose a game like that. The good ones show up at the park the next day like nothing happened, or better yet, as if they'd struck out the side the day before. Travis will be fine.

I got home late from the park. Patty woke up, and we stayed up until 2:30, assembling Easter baskets and crawling all over the apartment hiding Easter eggs. I suppose this is an annual routine in many homes. Not so for the Fireovids. This is the first time we've all been together on Easter. The boys have traveled more than most their age, although I wonder whether they'll remember enough of it to make it meaningful, to make it even begin to compensate for the absence of their father.

Sunday, April 15
Indianapolis

The boys found all the eggs in minutes, probably in seconds, far less time than Patty and I had taken to hide them. Then they sat cross-legged on the floor and tore through their Easter baskets, opening their New Kids on the Block bubble-gum cards and begging to eat their candy. Not until after church, Patty and I told them. Not until noon. We have a family rule: no sweets until afternoon.

We got all dressed up and went to church. Dressed up for us, anyway. We're not all that formal. Dressed up for the boys means that they weren't wearing sweatpants.

Of course, since it was Easter, the church was packed. And since we were with the kids, it was a given that we were running a little late. When we arrived, the church was full, every pew. We had to stand out in the vestibule, listening to the service on speakers mounted in the ceiling. The boys got restless and tired, and Patty and I took turns holding them, mainly to keep them separated. My back was killing me.

We went out to an Easter dinner afterward. Everything special about the day would have been ordinary for most people. To me it was extraordinary.

Randy Braun is off to a sad start. Coming into the season, he was penciled in as our regular first baseman. He had every reason to look forward to this year. He lives here in Indy, where he's an accountant during the off-season. On the last day of spring training, though, we acquired minor league veteran German Rivera, who, among other positions, plays first base. Randy hadn't been in a game for quite a while until this afternoon. Early in the game, on a weak ground ball, he sprained his ankle. He was forced to leave the game and is now on crutches.

Scott Anderson pitched another pearl today. Seven strong innings, allowing four hits and one run. The only problem is that we were shut out. He's now 0–1 on the season, with a microscopic earned run average. Let's say he gets roughed up the next time out. He's then 0–2 with a respectable ERA, instead of the 2–1 he should be. Pitchers have whole seasons like that, but as I said, Scott doesn't need one.

So far, Scott's not discouraged. He's been razor-sharp both times out, and wins will come along if he's able to stay in a groove.

We're now 3–5 and in last place in our division. Nobody who's ever played a full season would put any stock in standings this early in the year. There are lots of players and coaches, though, who love seeing Indianapolis at the bottom anytime they can. I always would have, except that they never were. Until now. Sometimes I think my entire career is an exercise in being in the right place at the wrong time.

Monday, April 16
Indianapolis

More bad news today for the Indians. James Steels broke his left thumb in four places sliding into second yesterday. We all thought he'd jammed his wrist or something, but he showed up today with a splint on his thumb. He had five hits in his last six at-bats and was swinging more the way I remember him in years past. It's a rotten break for James, any way you look at it.

Jim St. Laurent will get a chance to play now. He's only had two or three appearances at the plate this year, and it didn't look like he was on the verge of cracking the lineup anytime soon. James and Jim are both experienced minor league players. Nobody wanted James to get hurt, yet we're all glad to see Jim get some playing time. In his first at-bat today, Jim lined a ball off the opposing pitcher's chest. The pitcher recovered and threw him out. Jim came back to the dugout with a smile on his face and was heckled immediately. Jim's thick New England accent and his good-natured disposition invite verbal abuse whenever possible. Of course, he dishes it out, too. He's the type of person who goes up to the leadoff hitter, after the guy pops up the first pitch of the game, and asks, in a mock-serious way, what kind of stuff the pitcher has. If you don't have a sense of humor in this game, or can't take the ragging, you're a lonely man.

Tuesday, April 17
Indianapolis

This has been a long day. We had a businessman's special this afternoon, which is front-office language for a day game. Because of the cold weather, some teams schedule several of them early in the year.

They picked a perfect day. At two this afternoon, it was 40 degrees with 25-mile-per-hour winds at two. Fortunately it was blowing in from left. My game plan was simple. Pitch right-handers in and lefties away. There's no way anyone could have poked one out to left today.

I went seven innings, allowing an unearned run on five hits, striking out four and issuing two walks—my best effort to date. We beat Omaha 2–1, scoring once in the bottom of the ninth. Obviously I didn't get the win, but it was a positive outing nonetheless. I recorded four outs with my change-up and had a good feel for location.

Most pitchers wonder about their velocity after games. I don't want to know anymore. I don't believe velocity alone gets people out. Not only that, it flattens my ego when I do find out I was down in the low eighties.

I drove home after the game and surprised Patty. I needed some more stuff from the house, too. In fact, now it's really 6:30 A.M. on Wednesday in Bryan, Ohio. I want to get Joey around for school in a couple minutes. The boys were both asleep last night when I got home, so I'll only have an hour this morning with Joey. Sammy will be in my back pocket until

I leave for Indy this afternoon. I probably won't do this all the time, but it's nice to know that I can. It's worth the drive. Being three hours apart would be an ordeal for most families. For us, it's a pleasant change.

Wednesday, April 18
Indianapolis

We had ugly weather again tonight. We played an ugly game, too. We had no pitching, hitting, or defense and lost to Denver 6–2. Howard Farmer was on the mound for the third time this year, and for the third time he looked terrible. The playing conditions certainly did nothing to help stay limber, but there's speculation among some of the players that Howard has a sore arm and isn't telling anybody. He may feel he's only a small step away from the big leagues and doesn't want to jeopardize that. I can't tell if his arm's bothering him, because I didn't see him pitch much last year. Coming into this season, Howard probably is the number one prospect in Montreal's minor league system. I've seen many young players get off to shaky starts and never recover during the year. It's the mental aspect of the game that defeats most of them. However, three starts do not a season make.

Chris Marchok, the young Harvard grad, is confused. Three weeks ago he was comfortable. He'd been invited to big league camp and was the only lefthanded reliever with Indianapolis. He got in several games at first in crunch situations, throwing respectably. While we were shagging today, he told me he feels neglected now. "Nobody ever really works with me when I throw in the bullpen." I tried to remind him that relievers don't receive anywhere near the attention that starters do when throwing on the side. I don't think the lack of attention bothers Chris nearly as much as his lack of appearances. And I *know* it doesn't concern him as much as the arrival of Joe Olker, another lefthander, who showed up in uniform today.

Thursday, April 19
Indianapolis

Romy Cucjen is on fire so far this season. He's been disciplined at the plate and, when he gets a pitch to drive, he's been knocking the cover off the ball. He's been flawless in the field as well, playing either second or third base. He's second in the league in hitting and today socked a two-run homer to left.

You'd think if he kept this up the Expos would give him a call. Unfortunately, Romy has about as much of a chance at getting to the big leagues as I do. Don't misunderstand. I'm not implying that he can't maintain his current pace. We all hope he does. But he's not one of their prospects, one of their "boys." It'll take him months, not weeks, to raise an eyebrow in Montreal. Even then, it'd be because management was forced to be receptive due to a shortage of productivity up there. All Romy can do is try to stay on top of his game. Decisions in this business are not the cut-and-dry variety that many baseball fans believe. The cream does not always rise.

We scored ten runs today. It was great to see our guys put some hits together. We've been quiet offensively thus far. Scott Anderson is probably hoping we saved some for him tomorrow. He's had one run to work with in fourteen innings pitched. I've had two in seventeen.

Friday, April 20
Indianapolis

We got rained out tonight. They called it hours before game time. I went to the park, did my weights, and packed my bag for the six-day road trip we start tomorrow. I read for a while and then turned on the tube.

I watched a bit of the Cubs-Pirates game and saw a pitcher, Len Damien, that I beat twice last year walk two and give up a hit in relief before being lifted. He walked guys I've gotten out in the past. He was throwing to Rick Wrona, a catcher I've never had problems retiring. The opposing team's catcher, Mike LaValliere, was a backup with a Triple-A team I'd played on years ago.

And on and on it goes.

My phone's not hooked up yet, so I went to the store and called home. I came back and fixed something to eat. I turned the box on again. The Royals were getting beat by the Blue Jays, 17–6. I saw four different pitchers get hammered with pitches they deserved to get hammered with. I pitched with two of them, Luis Aquino and Steve Crawford, the past two seasons in Omaha. I know the Royals' pitching staff is much better than it showed tonight. It's one of the best in baseball. But I led their Triple-A team in wins both years I was with them and never got a sniff. In those two years, the Royals at one time or another called up thirteen pitchers. It would be easier to respect the Royals if I felt they'd respected me.

Saturday, April 21
Oklahoma City

I sat by Chris Marchok on the flight to Oklahoma City, and he showed me his travel guide. He has this thick catalogue which lists places of interest in the fifty states.

"There can't be much in there about Oklahoma City," I said. It is, I know, the home of the Cowboy Hall of Fame. Yee-ha. It's a good place, too, to buy rhinestone shirts and large Chevy belt buckles.

Chris shrugged. "Well, it is a little thin," he said, but he was bright-eyed all the same. He pointed his book at me. "This is the difference between you and me," he said.

I wondered which of the many differences between us he'd pick out: our age, our education, our pasts, our futures.

"Enthusiasm," Chris said.

More like realism, I thought. Chris is a type-A personality, often beneficial for a reliever, and I'm the definition of a type-B. But he's also not the kind of guy who sleeps until noon, orders room service, watches three soap operas, and heads out to the park. Chris spends a lot of days getting up early and taking a cab, alone, to some museum. You get the feeling Chris might have read a book without pictures in it.

Scott wasn't as sharp tonight as he'd been in his two previous starts, but he still kept us in the game, yielding three runs in six innings. We lost 7–2 and Scott is now 0–2 on the year. Needless to say, he's not real jovial at the moment.

Steve Smith is Oklahoma City's manager. He was also a teammate of mine in the Padres organization. I have so many friends who are now managers, coaches, or scouts. I look at some of them and wonder what they're doing still hanging around minor league ballparks. I'm sure some of them look at me and think, "Who's he kidding, still playing Triple-A baseball?"

Sunday April 22
Oklahoma City

We stink.

I thought of writing that a week ago, but I figured it was premature. It's mature now. I can safely say that the odds on a fifth consecutive league championship for the Indianapolis Indians are, in all honesty, long. We lost again this afternoon, again by a 7–2 score. Our pitching's been terrible and our hitting's been worse. We're small, we have no power, and we haven't been able to use what speed we have. Chemistry is vital in any team sport; this team has none. Tim Johnson chewed us out after the game and probably should have laid into us more than he did. I'm not writing us off, especially this early. But we're not a pretty sight.

Scott and I flipped on the TV tonight just in time for a special report on the Expos on ESPN. Montreal's made some noise because three of their current eight everyday players—Delino DeShields, Marquis Grissom, and Larry Walker—are rookies. Peter Gammons, ESPN's baseball analyst, then speculated about how Montreal would have to receive help from top prospects Howard Farmer and Mel Rojas, currently pitching at Indianapolis. He projected Howard to come up sometime in May and help the Expos contend. Baseball gurus think this is inevitable.

Scott and I looked at each other and laughed. Neither of us doubt that Howard can be a winning major league pitcher. His future is promising. It's nothing personal, either. The plain and simple truth is that right now Howard and Mel are struggling big time, while Scott and I are throwing well. We laugh, but we don't find the story funny. We laugh because we've been around long enough to know it doesn't do any good to cry. We also laugh at Peter Gammons, because half the time the experts don't have a clue. Their forecast is partially correct, though, concerning Howard and Mel. If they pitch well at all, any openings in Montreal are theirs.

Monday, April 23
Oklahoma City

We avoided the sweep tonight, winning 4–3. We fell behind 3–0, but scored twice in the fifth and sixth to go ahead and then held it from there. I went eight innings, walking four and striking out two. The walks are beginning to upset me. I normally walk four in two or three games—not eight innings. I wanted to finish it, but evidently I was well over a hundred pitches, and Joe decided that was enough.

The fourth inning really got under my skin. I'll admit when I have nothing or tip my cap when I have good stuff and get knocked around. The three runs they scored off me in the fourth were ugly. The cleanup hitter, Mike Berger, lifted a lazy fly ball over Romy's head at third. Berger's a lefthanded hitter and he hit it three or four inches from his hands. Two runs in. The third run scored when Andy Allanson, their six-four, 225-pound catcher, laid down a bunt—with two outs—to "drive" in the man from third. That got my goat. It only bothered me because it worked, though.

We're securely locked in last place, three games behind Buffalo. We head to Denver tomorrow morning and have a three-game series there. It'll be kind of a vacation for me. I actually work harder physically the three days after I throw than the day I pitch, but it's brain-dead work for the most part, and it doesn't drain me. The altitude in Denver kills any desire I have to run distance anyway. I look forward to Denver; for some reason, a bunch of high school buddies of mine have moved out here to find themselves. Not only that, it's a fun town. I don't need Marchok's travel guide to know that.

Tuesday, April 24
Denver

We played the sloppiest game I've seen in years tonight. It went ten innings and came only five minutes short of being a four-hour affair. We committed three errors. Our pitchers walked ten and struck out two, plus, for good measure, hit a batter. We had five pitchers partake in the fiasco. Howard started and went three frames, allowing seven runs. It has to be so frustrating for him because his ability is *so* apparent, yet he's been unable to tap it thus far. Confidence can overcome so many minor complications on the mound. Howard's confidence is nil.

There was one positive side tonight, though: we pounded Denver for seventeen hits en route to a 14–11 victory.

One quick story from tonight's game. Denver's starting pitcher, was getting lit up and decided he'd had enough. That's understandable. When he could take it no longer, he fired a fastball up and in at one of our hitters. That, too, is understandable. But then, like some cartoon bull with steam shooting out of his nostrils, he strutted toward home plate, stabbed the return throw from the catcher with his bare throwing hand, and slammed it against his cup while staring at the hitter. Scott and I thought it a rather juvenile attempt at intimidation and bust out laughing up in the stands.

Jose Castro went to the hospital last night in Oklahoma City with the chicken pox. He's been sicker than a dog the last couple of days. It's of major concern to all of us here.

Wednesday, April 25
Denver

Game time was twelve-thirty-five today. We had to be dressed at ten-thirty, and after the marathon we played last night it seemed like we never left Mile High Stadium. Batting practice was rained out for the second straight day here. Denver doesn't feature ideal baseball weather this time of the year. It seems like none of the towns in this league do.

We lost 6–4. Mel Rojas started for us. Mel's the other pitcher Montreal is keeping a close eye on. He's a five-eleven Dominican righthander with good baseball genes: he's the nephew of Felipe, Jesus, and Matty Alou. As soon as he gets on a roll here, he's going to be an Expo. There's a couple kids at Double-A, too, Chris Nabholz and Brian Barnes, who Montreal has their eyes on. But Mel, like Howard, is still looking for his first strong outing. He fought his control throughout the game today, walking seven in six innings, while yielding four runs. Mel's out pitch is his forkball, and he has a nasty one, but he hasn't been ahead in the count often enough this year to use it with the frequency he'd like. This early in the season, earned run averages and batting averages are poor gauges of a player's performance. At best, they give you an idea of who's hot and who's not. Through four starts, Howard's ERA is in the 8's, Mel's is somewhere in the 6's, and mine is 2.49.

Today Montreal put lefthanded (and thirty-one-year-old) reliever Joe Hesketh on waivers. As May approaches, teams are beginning to reduce their rosters. There will be changes made here and on down the ladder. Nobody here knows what'll happen, but most everybody is voicing opinions on what *could* take place.

Personally, I'm not worried too much about my fate here. I'm off to a sound start. If *my* ERA were floating in the 8's, I'd be shaking in my boots. In a nutshell, that's the difference between a prospect and a suspect.

Thursday, April 26
Denver

The pitchers had a meeting with Joe Kerrigan today before batting practice. He didn't assemble us to applaud our collective effort, either. We suck. More specifically, we're all allowing far too many walks, especially of the two-out variety. He said some of us are pitching scared and that, if those concerned don't become more aggressive immediately, roster decisions will be easy to make in a few days. It was short and to the point and not the least bit sugar-coated. It was also needed.

We put on an offensive display tonight, mashing twenty-one hits and winning 14–2. We won three and lost three on the trip. The rule of thumb is that if you can win half your games on the road, you can contend. Scott was the beneficiary of our output tonight, notching his first win of the year. After eighteen games, we're back to .500.

We wake up at 5 A.M. to get back to Indy for a three-game series against Oklahoma City. Luckily, it's over the weekend, so Patty and the boys can drive down after Joey gets out of school. She figures that, if all goes well, they'll get into Indy at about five-thirty. We'll almost certainly have batting practice, which means I'll have to be dressed and on the field at four-thirty. She told me to put them on the pass list for the game, just in case the boys' persistence wins out. Odds are I'll drive

54

to the apartment after the game and spend a little time with them there if they're still awake. I'll be tired from my long day and, since I'm pitching the next day, I'll need to get to bed.

People should avoid using the words "glamour" and "baseball" in the same breath around Patty, especially in her present condition.

Friday, April 27
Indianapolis

I wasn't totally correct about today's schedule; there were a couple pleasant surprises today. Our connecting flight was on time from Chicago. That's rare. Tim Johnson then announced there would be no batting practice. We didn't have to be dressed until six. My family pulled up to the apartment just as I was leaving, so we had ten minutes together before I had to go. We spent our time hauling stuff in from the car and convincing Joey that we already *had* a shortstop. When I got back from the game, at about eleven, they were sound asleep.

We had a large crowd tonight at Bush Stadium. That can mean only one thing: some trinket's being given away. I had a new coffee mug in my locker; that must have been the drawing card. Coffee mug night. They could give away year-old calendars and people would flock to the turnstiles.

The crowd, as a bonus, witnessed an outstanding game. We won 1–0. I say witnessed instead of enjoyed because most fans would rather see a 10–9 game with pitchers serving up five-hundred-foot blasts from start to finish. We used four pitchers to piece together the shutout.

We seem to be playing a lot better since I said we stunk.

I'll gladly stand corrected.

The boys will be up bright and early and they won't want to hear about my being tired, so I'd best get some sleep, too.

Saturday, April 28
Indianapolis

We beat Oklahoma City again tonight, 5–1. The team is beginning to take on an identity. Maybe the players are finally getting used to each other. I had my best outing of the season. I threw the first complete game of the year for us, giving up six hits, walking one and striking out five. I picked up my tempo a little, which in turn gave me less time to think between pitches.

I may have been a bit too calculated on the mound before. I really don't have the power or the assortment to justify heavy thought out there. As humbling as it is to my brain, I'm better off as a robot than an Einstein. I broke three or four bats and had a ton of ground balls. Another encouraging sign was that I threw only 104 pitches. I didn't issue the walk until one out in the ninth, and I followed that up with a game-ending double-play ball.

Nights like tonight provide a glimmer of hope for me. Years ago, after pitching like I did tonight, I'd be much more consumed in the effort. I'd experience personal gratification for sure, but more important was the attention I just *knew* I was getting at the next level. I don't feel it anymore. I take a lot of pride in what I do and will forever believe I belong in the big leagues. My believing it, or my proving it, is hardly reciprocated by the major leagues, though. So while I sense that glimmer now, I also know how much is out of my control.

Sunday, April 29
Indianapolis

Howard Farmer came through today. He worked eight innings and allowed three runs, walked one, and struck out nine. Everybody knew it was only a matter of time before he made a strong showing. It should do wonders for his confidence.

Jim St. Laurent was released after the game. He was a funny addition to our clubhouse and we'll miss him. The time had come, though, for rosters to be reduced and something—someone—had to give. Jim knew his days here might be numbered. He talked about it often, and I could tell it was bothering him. In a way, he's probably glad it's over, provided he can latch on with another team. That won't be easy. Right now, there are thirty or forty players in the same boat, begging for jobs.

We got our bimonthly checks today. We have a nice house in Bryan to maintain plus the $700 a month it costs us for utilities, telephone, furniture, and rent at the apartment in Indy. There's food, gas, and all the necessary expenses for both residences as well. Come July, there'll be another child entering the picture. We're not to be pitied financially, but I'd like to stress that we're not to be envied either.

We have the day off tomorrow so Patty and I each took a child and drove home to Bryan after the game. I'll do some work around the house, play with the boys, and hopefully see a couple of people about job possibilities after the season. At this point, I can't put it off.

May

Tuesday, May 1
Buffalo

I've had a busy day today. I woke up at 5 A.M. in Bryan and, fueled as much by coffee as gasoline, drove the three hours back to Indianapolis, just in time to catch the flight to Buffalo with the team. I'd hoped to catch a couple hours of sleep on the plane, but then the coffee turned on me. I was wired. Still, I figured that, once we landed, I'd go grab a couple hours in the rack before going to the park. Wrong again. Joe Kerrigan suggested that, since it was my day to throw on the side, I go directly from the airport to the stadium. What am I going to say? "No thanks, Joe. I really don't feel like bettering myself this afternoon." So off I went to the park, bleary-eyed and whipped.

Les Straker's day was worse than mine. He was released this morning. It came as a surprise to everyone. We knew we were still one over our allotted roster, but nobody expected it would be Les. He started a few days ago and was brilliant. He was a starter for the Twins the year they won the World Series. They had nursed his arm along since spring training and now that he's ready, he's gone. Funny game.

61

We had a 4–1 lead entering the bottom of the eighth tonight and gave up six runs, finally losing 7–5. Travis Chambers's season has been a nightmare so far. He failed to hold the lead again and after the game sat in the bottom of a locker and stared at the ball. Just sat there and stared, like it was going to talk to him, like it was going to give him some answers. You watch Travis throw in the bullpen and wonder how *anyone* can hit his slider. But now he's messed up mentally, and that's a rut not easily overcome. He feels like everyone's staring at him. Maybe we are; we don't know what to say. Joe Kerrigan, though, had something to say to him, behind closed doors.

Wednesday, May 2
Buffalo

Chris Marchok is a frustrated young man. He hasn't pitched in a game for seven days—an eternity if you're designated as the lefthander to be used in the late innings. Twice in the past week, Chris has been ready in the pen, only to watch as we put in a righthander to face a lefthanded batter. It goes against the conventional rules of baseball, but I'm not here to judge managerial decisions—and I'm not going to start. Chris just wants to know why he's not being called upon to perform.

The pitchers had another little get-together today with Joe Kerrigan and Tim Johnson. Tim said he's through with character-building appearances for the relievers and then outlined each of their roles. That was probably directed at Travis. He finished up by saying that he doesn't owe any explanations to anyone on how he uses the bullpen. *That* was definitely directed at Chris. So Chris got his answer after all: there will *be* no answer.

We won 6–1 today. Scott went the distance for us, picking up his second win. We've had ten outings between the two of us, and they've all been quality starts. It helps to have some friendly competition within the staff. Younger players tend to feel threatened by a teammate's success. The more experienced guys understand the politics of the game more and generally pull for anyone to beat the odds. There's no reason for any jealousy between us anyway. We're both turds.

Thursday, May 3
Buffalo

The Bisons beat us 3–2 in the series finale this afternoon. We were behind 1–0 going into the bottom of the seventh. I retired the first man, but the next guy doubled. The following batter was a lefty, and I was relieved by none other than Chris. Buffalo countered with a pinch hitter. Chris craftily got the gut to hit a bullet at our third baseman for the second out. Then, though, Chris gave up a line drive over the third baseman's head and the run scored. They scored again in the eighth and we pushed two runs across in the ninth to come within one.

I struck out only one and didn't walk anybody. They collected nine hits off me, although six of those were ground balls that scooted through the infield. The drawback to being a ground-ball pitcher—as opposed to a strikeout artist—is that I can do what I set out to do, get the hitters to hit the ball on the ground, and if the defense behind me is spotty, or the grounders have eyes, I'll still give up a lot of hits. A strikeout pitcher doesn't have to leave nearly as much to chance. Physically I was fine throughout the game. I wasn't real pleased with my control. Even though I didn't give up any walks, I threw several pitches that were way too fat in the strike zone. I can't get away with pitching like that.

I don't know too many people who like to lose. I'm poor at it; I space out, or get so wired that I'm hardly aware of what's going on in the room—or even what room I'm in. I went through the complete three-stage procedure of cleaning my contacts before I realized they were still in my eyes. Athletes aren't the only people subject to such intensity, obviously. I hate losing, but I'm thankful for a job that can provoke that kind of emotion. It lets me know I'm alive.

Friday, May 4
Indianapolis

I found out, when we got to the airport last night, that Joe Olker was released. He joined us a couple weeks ago, and I can only remember him pitching in one game. I didn't get a chance to talk to him, but I heard that the release caught him off guard. Scott spent some time with him and said Joe was particularly upset because, even though other teams had expressed interest, he'd chosen the Expos, thinking there was more opportunity here. The timing's terrible for Joe, since the roster reductions just went into effect, and there's dozens of players in his shoes. Phones are ringing off the hook all over the country with unemployed baseball players looking for jobs. I know the feeling.

We were some kind of flat tonight. Howard wasn't sharp on the mound, we made four errors, and, after the game, Tim and Joe weren't in cordial moods. Nashville whipped us 8–4, dropping us farther behind them and first-place Buffalo.

John Boles came to town today for the homestand. I found out about his visit when I walked in the clubhouse this afternoon, and several guys told me my dad's here. I knew instantly who they were talking about. That's common terminology for a someone in a powerful position who likes a particular player. Hopefully I'll get a chance to chat with John while he's here.

Saturday, May 5
Indianapolis

Rich Thompson came down from Montreal today. Rich and I are friends, and, although it's great to see him, it's unfortunate it has to be under these circumstances. He'd been with the Expos for the past month and pitched one inning. Right now, he'd be a lousy character witness for this organization. What happened to him is sickening. It's also personally disheartening; I can see myself in his shoes. And now, for a while, I guess, we'll be in the same shoes.

Rich is a fellow turd. Neither of us makes scouts' jaws drop when they see our little blips on the radar gun. Our days of velocity in the 90's are long gone—too bad for us, since Montreal puts a lot of emphasis on rushing it to the plate. We're both righthanded ground-ball pitchers who strike out few but walk many fewer. Our combined age would get you a senior citizen discount at McDonald's.

Last year, Rich had the lowest ERA in this league. He put together the type of year pitchers dream of. He was the model of consistency and was the workhorse of this Indianapolis staff, which was by far the best around. He wasn't their most dynamic pitcher, "only" their most dependable. He was called up in July and threw well for Montreal over the remainder of the season. He was solid in spring training for them this year, too, and rightly felt optimistic about his status. They rewarded him with one inning and a demotion to Indy, where, to rub salt in the wound, he'll be in the bullpen because there's no room for him here in our starting rotation.

So what happens if *I* have a career year this season? Anything? I'm aware that I'll never find out unless I pitch exceptionally well, and I'm working my tail off to do just that. But then I look at how Rich, a guy who's resume looks a lot like mine, has been dogged, and it's hard for me to shrug off. Then again, he just spent a month in the big leagues.

Sunday, May 6
Indianapolis

We broke our three-game losing streak this afternoon, beating Nashville 4–2. Rich picked up the win in relief of Mel Rojas, who pitched well during his six innings. In three of his four starts, Mel's shown why Montreal holds him in such high regard. When he's right, his forkball simply *disappears* at the plate.

Rick Williams joined us today. As overseer of the Expos' minor league pitching, Rick spends much of his time traveling from one farm club to another. So we now have both John Boles and Rick in town. Several little Indians wonder whether something's up.

The only thing I see that's up is Howard's ERA. I know that's disturbing to Montreal. Today was his day to throw on the side between starts, and, between Joe Kerrigan and Rick, the kid was put under a microscope. Joe has the best eye for flaws in a delivery I've ever seen, so it's difficult to imagine what it's like to be double-teamed by those guys for a half-hour. But it's possible that Joe and Rick are feeling a little anxious, too. There's a lot of pressure on coaches when a "can't miss" kid is missing. Joe's proven his worth to this organization, though. On the other hand, he works so hard and takes too much pride in his abilities not to agonize over a student's struggles. Some coaches would ease off, hoping the pitcher bounces back on his own. Joe has too much confidence in himself to take that approach. It'll be a "hands-on" process until Howard comes out of it.

Patty and the boys arrived here yesterday around noon and left today at about the same time. We had three hours together yesterday before I went to work and a couple this morning before I had to leave. She drove six hours, three each way, so we could spend five hours together as a family. Her body isn't designed for traveling right now, either; she's seven months pregnant and she had to tilt the steering wheel all the way up just to fit in the driver's seat. All this while trying to keep one eye on the road and the other on Joey and Sammy, who usually spend the trip bouncing around in the backseat, losing crayons, begging for drinks, and fighting over the volume knob on their tape player. Once she gets to Indy, she volunteers to make the meals and otherwise runs the ship. She'd be the last person to complain, but this morning as I watched her drive away, I felt guilty for putting her through all this.

Monday, May 7
Indianapolis

Scott Anderson had his first subpar outing of the year tonight, giving up five runs in six innings against division-leading Buffalo. We lost the game 5–4 and are now back to playing .500 baseball. My locker is next to Dale Mohorcic's. Anyone who's familiar with Horse knows he has a no-nonsense approach to life. He has to be one of the most genuine people I know. After the game, I went into this long-winded analysis of all that might be wrong with us and why. He listened quietly. When I was done, he nodded, looked me in the eye, and offered me his condensed version: "We're not very good."

Danny Clay had a rough night. He's been our best reliever this season and has been used in every possible situation. He appeared in tonight's game and was again perfect. He lives in Columbus, Ohio, and made the trip home after yesterday's afternoon game.

It's a three-hour drive home for him, too, and he was awfully tired today at the yard. After the game, he found out that two tires had been stolen off his truck in Bush Stadium's parking lot. I went with him to check it out. Sure enough, the truck was up on blocks; the lug nuts were gone, too, so the spares that other players offered were useless.

He went up to the Indians' office to file a report with the police. I couldn't believe how composed he was; maybe he was just too tired to flip out.

Bush Stadium's not located in the nicest part of town, and we think whoever did it may come back in the middle of the night to finish the job.

This is another reminder of where we are. Jose Canseco's tires aren't tampered with while he's playing. If they ever were, he might issue some brash threat in the headlines or open a 900 number for clues on his assailant. The next time you're so irritated by some multimillionaire's ego that you're tempted to tar all ballplayers with the same brush, remember Danny Clay's tires.

Thursday, May 8
Indianapolis

I stunk tonight. I lasted only five innings and gave up seven runs, five of which were earned. I served up my first longball of the year in the process. I didn't walk anyone, but that was probably only because they were so anxious to tee off on me. Five days ago, I was victimized by a lot of ground-ball hits. I can't offer any excuses tonight. Six of the seven hits were rockets. I now know our outfielders' uniform numbers; I spent the night with my back to the plate, watching them chase balls. On the bright side, I kept my strikeout streak alive. I fanned one.

Joe spoke with me in the tunnel before I headed to the showers. He said tonight could be a positive outing if I would allow it to be. He'd suggested a change in my delivery a few days ago, hoping it'd add some velocity to my fastball. They had me at 88 mph on the gun, and Joe was pleased with the improvement, stating, "In the long run, I'm convinced it'll make you a better pitcher."

If Joe's convinced, I believe it, too. The only problem I see is that, unless I get back to the big leagues, this may very well be my final year. I don't have much time to tinker with adjustments. My career will have no "long run" if this isn't a correction I can make in short order. I'm going to stick with it, though, because I'm positive Joe knows what he's doing. I should add that it's a subtle change that I should be able to handle. He didn't ask that I try throwing lefthanded.

I called home afterward. By now, Patty has heard it all. She doesn't don pom-poms when games go well, and she doesn't break out the Kleenex when I get shelled. Sammy, though, will take it personally. He showers me with good-luck kisses, and when I lose, he feels that somehow his kisses were deficient. When Joey hears, he'll say "that's too bad," and then in the same breath ask if I got him any new G.I. Joe men.

Wednesday, May 9
Indianapolis

The day after you get shelled is a day to get through. Baseball is a humbling profession, and last night I got a heaping helping of humility. But I'm experienced enough to know how much of this game is mental. So I woke up this morning and did my daily sit-ups and push-ups. I resented them a little more than usual, but I did them. I wasn't as eager to show my face at Bush Stadium, the scene of the crime, but I forced myself to go early and run five or six miles—my custom on days after I pitch, good outing or bad. Then Joe and Rick put me on the mound and we went through some more modifications in my windup. The best antidote for defeat is to work the attitude right back into shape.

Today I got a chance to speak briefly with John Boles. We spoke in the showers; it's the only place in our cramped and crumbling clubhouse that's at all private. "How seriously," I asked, "does this organization take me, as a pitcher, as a player?"

He rinsed the soap off his face, turned to me, and paused. "They think you're all right," he said.

That's about what I thought he'd say. I've been around long enough, and I know John well enough, that I hardly expected him to say how much the Expos cherish my astonishing talents.

"Fire, what I'm waiting for," John said, "is the day when you come up to me and tell me that this year will be your last, so I can offer you a pitching-coach job."

I didn't have much to say about that. I don't know if I'd be a good coach, I *do* know I'd be reluctant to live a coach's life-style, and I *definitely* know that I can't dwell on any of this now.

I toweled off, and that was pretty much the end of our con-versation. We'd both had my career in mind. I wanted to know how it was being looked upon and he (or John) wanted to know when it would be cast aside.

We lost again tonight and finished the homestand with one win and five losses. We may stink more than when I originally wrote we stunk. We leave for Louisville and Nashville tomorrow morning, so maybe the change will do us some good. It can't hurt.

Thursday, May 10
Louisville

We boarded the bus at nine this morning for the two-hour drive to Louisville. I don't mind short bus trips at all, and it doesn't bother me in the least to share a seat with somebody. Yester-day, though, I was up late and I *wanted* both seats. This is my usual technique.

First, I arrive early enough to get an aisle seat. This way, anyone who wants to join me will have to ask. Next I place my carry-on bag on the seat by the window. Then I pretend to be asleep, open mouth and all. Guys walk right by. Yesterday, even Horse fell for it. "Shoot," he said. "Fire's already asleep." Everyone knows how rude it is to wake someone up. Once I feel the bus move, I remove my pillow from my bag, prop it against the window, and stretch out. Works every time.

We lost 4–1 this evening to last-place Louisville. I think they're only a game behind us now. I tried to convince Romy Cucjen to call a team meeting tomorrow.

Right now, a pitcher can't really call a meeting. It has to be one of the everyday players. We seem to be without a leader on the field. Romy has the respect of the players but doesn't picture himself as leader material. Someone has to step forward, though. We've lost eight of our last ten, and we're accepting defeats way too easily, almost in stride.

We did make national news tonight, sort of. Scott and I got back to the room and watched a little ESPN. After recapping the St. Louis Cardinals game, Chris Berman pointed out that Ken Hill, a pitcher on their Triple-A club in Louisville, struck out fifteen in seven innings. Berman, bless him, didn't mention that it came against us.

Friday, May 11
Louisville

We had a team meeting today before batting practice. With the manager and coaches out of the clubhouse, players can speak their minds. We don't have anyone on this team who has a loud personality, though, so it wound up being a low-key discussion. We talked for a while about how aggressive we aren't. Then the big issue came up: because of all the roster moves this organization's been making, people are playing scared. We still have five players on the disabled list, and more than a few of the active players are worried that they'll be gone the second the injured guys heal. We all agreed that we're not having any fun playing the game—although it's impossible to have fun when you're losing all the time. If we were having fun now we'd be accused of lacking professionalism. We talked for a while longer and eventually finished the way all these meetings finished: we agreed we all had to turn it up a notch.

The pitchers also met with Joe. It was a Pitching 101 class, emphasizing the simplicity of pitch selection in various situations. Joe, too, brought up our collective lack of aggressiveness and abundance of fear. Joe promised (not to be confused with threatened) he wouldn't tolerate guys pitching scared much longer.

All this wasn't enough to snap us out of our slump. We lost

3–1 and are now tied with Louisville for last place in our division, seven games behind Buffalo. We'll try to avoid another series sweep tomorrow. Tim Johnson has called off batting practice, infield, and everything else in preparation for the game. The bus leaves the hotel at 6:15 for a 7:15 game. It'll be like the old American Legion days. Strap 'em on and go.

Saturday, May 12
Louisville

For about fifteen minutes tonight, we looked like a team of destiny. We had only two hits through six innings and trailed Louisville 4–0. We scored twice in the seventh, followed with one in the eighth, and finished with two more in the ninth to take a 5–4 lead. Rich Thompson came in to preserve the win for us. Our bench was actually alive in anticipation of a win. The optimism lasted one pitch. Rich's second pitch sailed out of the park, tying the game.

The remainder of the inning went like this: single, sacrifice bunt, intentional walk, balk, another intentional walk, sacrifice fly. We lost 6–5.

Rich, ordinarily a composed guy, just snapped. He threw bats, he threw his glove, he threw his spikes, his face went red, he invented a few new cuss words—the whole package. There's a feeling coming over this team that this losing streak is bigger than any of us. We're now busing to Nashville, where we'll play two games.

Up in the bigs, the Expos have been playing good baseball so far this season, much to the surprise of all the "experts." It doesn't come as a shock to any of us who know the game, though. I know Montreal is keeping an eye on our catcher, Jerry Goff, but other than him, I don't see any reason for anyone down here to wait by the phone. Right now, Oil Can Boyd's arm is all messed up again, and they may find themselves looking for a starter soon. My guess is they'd either move a reliever into the rotation or make a trade for someone. If Howard throws at all well, though, he could be the answer.

Some naive soul might think Montreal would just dip down into its system and bring up the starter who's having the best season.

I'm not a naive soul, and I'm not going anywhere.

Sunday, May 13
Nashville

The streak is over at last. We beat Nashville this afternoon, 4–0. I started and went seven innings before being lifted for a pinch hitter. Horse came in and finished them off. The new delivery felt more comfortable this time, but I had better concentration, too, which was probably more significant. I gave up three hits, struck out three, and didn't issue any walks. My velocity was again up from my pre-Kerrigan norm, topping out at 89. I'm inching my way back to the 90's. Velocity isn't an area most pitchers seek to improve, simply because there's very little that can be done about it. It makes no difference to hitters if I throw 89 or 90. Neither is overpowering. It does, however, seem to be a standard of measure to this organization.

Jerry Goff is going to the big leagues. It was announced after today's game. My first thought was that nobody will believe I wrote about that possibility yesterday. When you've been around a while, though, you develop a feel for such matters. Maybe I should be a coach after all.

The pitchers are having an early workout tomorrow and another one the following day. That one will hurt. It's an off day (one of only nine in the entire season), and I was planning to go home. Today is Mother's Day, and I've again spent it away from Patty, as well as away from my own mom. I had hoped to take Patty and the boys out for a belated Mother's Day dinner Tuesday night. Maybe if we win again tomorrow Joe will call off Tuesday's workout. But that's less a hunch than it is wishful thinking.

Monday, May 14
Nashville

All the pitchers left the motel at one-thirty today for the early workout with Joe. We pulled on our spikes and met Joe on the mound. We also grabbed our cups; Joe's been known to vent his wrath through a fungo bat during pitchers' fielding practice. "I don't care what you guys want to call this," Joe said. "If you think it's punishment, that's fine. If you think it's horseshit, that's okay with me, too. But I'm not going to sit back and watch you 'fellows' continue to give the other team thirty outs when they only need twenty-seven to beat us."

Obviously, we weren't gathered this afternoon to go through the motions.

We ran through the standard drills with more than standard intensity and concluded the session with "comebackers." Many coaches, such as Rick Williams, are artists with a fungo, hitting the ball wherever they choose with whatever velocity they want. Joe Kerrigan wouldn't fall into this category. However, what he lacks in direction, he makes up for in bat-speed. Marchok was bruised twice on the same grounder. Horse has a baseball-sized welt a couple inches south of the border. After it was all over, the starters battled the relievers in a simulated game, with Joe as the pitcher. My softball days paid dividends in the outfield, where I made one diving catch and caught another off the wall.

I then ran five miles, did my weights, shagged batting practice, showered, and went up in the stands with the radar gun. I sat next to a Yankee scout. A couple innings into the game, the guy leaned over to me. "You know how to pitch," he whispered. "You belong in the major leagues." I've heard that stuff for years, and I'm way past the point of being flattered.

Howard threw for us tonight and pitched pretty well, but we lost 5–4 anyway. Did I mention that we stink?

Tuesday, May 15
Bryan, Ohio

Last night on the bus trip back to Indianapolis, I tried to sleep on the bus but didn't have much success. Joe announced that the workout scheduled for today was off, and so, when we arrived back at Bush Stadium, even though it was 4 A.M., I was tempted to go straight home to Bryan. I fell asleep, though, as Horse gave me a ride to my apartment in Indy, and I knew I didn't have it in me. I slept until nine, hopped in the car, and drove home to Bryan. I stopped on the way and picked up some flowers for the Mother's Day we never had and surprised Patty.

Then it was time to pick up Joey from school. He was happy to see me, but he had to be cool in front of friends, too, which allows only so much affection. He was all smiles, although there's not that much smile to see; he lost his other front tooth since I last saw him. Our next stop was Sammy's school. Joey insisted on going in to fetch his brother, promising to keep Daddy's presence a secret. He was only gone a few seconds so he may not have had enough time to spill his guts. When I first saw Sammy, he was walking, just another day at school. Then he saw me. He broke into a dead sprint, his arms flailing and his face covered by this huge grin. The four of us drove home together like normal families do at the end of normal days.

The boys and I played Superman, with me cast as Lex Luthor. The boys are too big for Patty to play rough with anymore, and she's too big herself these days to wrestle. I gave Patty the night off from cooking and again burnt the burgers on the grill. The boys keep asking me when I have to leave again. This time it's not so bad, though, because they'll be coming to Indy over the weekend.

I got a chance to see my parents, too. Mom had a series of

tests yesterday; the doctors had suspected cancer. She found out today the tests were negative, and, of course, she didn't let us know anything at all until today, until the news was good. That's my mom for you.

Wednesday, May 16
Indianapolis

It's been a busy day. I woke up with Joey this morning to get him ready for school and then I made the beds and did the dishes. When Patty and Sammy woke up, we watched the video of his preschool class's musical production. They acted out "I'm a Little Teapot" and "Ten Little Indians." Sammy was the ninth little Indian. His dad was the out-of-town big Indian. I seldom get a chance to see the boys' activities during the season, and it means a lot to Sammy. The rest of the morning we ran errands, and, all too soon, it was time to take Sammy to school and leave for Indy. He wanted to be held all morning and I cooperated as long as my arms could bear it. Most five-year-old boys probably don't ask to be held that much, but most don't have part-time fathers either.

I drove directly from Bryan to the stadium, just in time for another early workout for the pitchers, which was supposed to take the place of the one we didn't have yesterday. We went over the fundamentals. Once, while covering bunts down the third-base line, I scooped the ball up with my glove instead of both hands. "Two hands, Fire," Joe said, without any real annoyance. When I came back to wait my turn at the end of the line, Howard shook his head in disbelief. "If I ever did that," Howard said, "he'd be all over me. He'd make me do another one or make me do extra work after we're done."

Howard's not allowed to get out of line, no matter how trivial the transgression. What he may not realize, though, is that you discipline those you care about. That doesn't mean Joe cares nothing for me, but Howard has both the tools *and* the age to justify high expectations from Montreal, and they want him as finely tuned as possible. It's tough for Howard to appreciate his situation, especially as he's struggling. He feels smothered by the attention. "I wish they'd leave me alone," he told me as we were running. If he got his wish, *then* he'd truly have something to worry about.

Thursday, May 17
Indianapolis

My agent, Jim Bronner, called today to check on me. We discussed the usual stuff at first, which means statistics. I'm not a close follower of stats, but they are the only indicator to those removed from the actual game. Currently, I'm leading the league in innings pitched (fifty-three) and have the third lowest ERA at 2.56. Jim was pleased but he also knows it doesn't mean a whole lot. I've put up good numbers before without anything to show for it, so we've adapted a laid-back attitude toward my returning to the big leagues. We joked about how everyone here feels I'll be a coach someday except me, spoke of whether that might affect their opinions of me as a player. I feel like a dormant volcano that still has lava. Jim then introduced an intriguing idea. Japan. He feels they may be interested in me for next year. He warned that it's a difficult market. He didn't have to tell me not to get my hopes up, though. After the career I've had so far, I never do, and he knows I won't.

We split a doubleheader with Louisville tonight. We're still in last place, eight games behind Buffalo. Jose Castro is over the chicken pox, but Mel Rojas and German Rivera are now infected. We still have four catchers and eight relievers. The disabled list seems to change from day to day. We must be at least three players over the limit, even including those who are sick and injured. Nobody's really sure. It's going to get ugly around here when everybody gets healthy.

Players are scared. Travis Chambers is even considering what classes he should take when he returns to college—this summer.

Friday, May 18
Indianapolis

I had nothing tonight on the mound. I didn't feel real sharp mentally, and it was obvious I wasn't strong physically. My fastball was back down to 86–87. I was lifted with two outs in the seventh, having given up two runs, both in the first inning. Louisville collected nine hits off me in addition to the walk I gave them. I failed to strike out anybody; I was fooling no one. I was fortunate to get away with only two runs against me. We lost, 5–1.

Tim Johnson couldn't take it anymore. We'd been expecting him to blow, and tonight he burst. He walked in the clubhouse, looked around the room, and headed for the food table. "That's horseshit baseball," he said, loud enough for everyone to hear. He grabbed a platter of french fries and let them fly. We just sat there. We deserve more wrath than that, and we know it. The fans are booing us, and we're tempted to boo ourselves.

Jose Castro got up and threw one of the french fries at Wild Bill. "Your food sucks anyway," Jose said.

Patty came up for the weekend. She got to the apartment minutes after I left for the park. I talked to her on the phone and we'd planned to get a pizza tonight. But the game got too long, the boys got too tired, and Patty's too pregnant to deal with it. By the time I got back to the apartment, they were all asleep. The boys had pitched a tent on the living room floor and they were bundled up there, in a pile of blankets, pretending they were Lewis and Clark or something. Patty was sacked out in the bedroom.

I made myself a frozen pizza, sat on the couch, near the tent, and had dinner alone, by the light of the TV.

Saturday, May 19
Indianapolis

I'd like to expand a little bit on a seemingly insignificant episode that took place in the stands during last night's game. First, allow me to introduce the cast. Scott was up in the crowd operating the radar gun, which we all do the day after a start. Righthander John Costello is down here from Montreal on a rehab assignment. Finally, Dave Dombrowski, general manager of the Montreal Expos, is in town to observe us.

First, Scott monitored John on the chart. As John threw his scheduled inning of relief last night, he struck a hitter out and Dave came over to Scott and asked how hard the pitch was.

"Eighty-three," Scott said.

Dave looked over Scott's shoulder at the chart. John's fastball had topped out at 87 for the evening. "That must be that new grip he's trying out," Dave said.

Today, Costello told Scott it was just a fastball he guided to the plate.

The point is this. Even in an organization where velocity supposedly means a lot, exceptions get made. John was acquired this spring in a trade from St. Louis and *will* pitch in the major leagues for Montreal. His 83- to 87-mph fastball—slower than *mine*—can be overlooked. This isn't anything against Costello or Dombrowski. It's how the game works. If another club traded a big league player for me tomorrow, I'd be treated with utmost respect by my new team, too.

Sunday, May 20
Indianapolis

Before the game today, we had another team meeting. This time it was called by Dave Stewart, who's a nutrition and positive-thinking specialist employed by the Expos—kind of a cross between Norman Vincent Peale and Richard Simmons. He wanted with all his heart to get to the root of our problems as a team and help bring us out of our slump. He also, naively, volunteered to be a sounding board between the players and the coaching staff. That's about the same as warning us not to confide in him if we have any serious complaints.

I felt sorry for him. Our team's problems go deeper than low-fiber diets and negative visualization, and the guys weren't responsive to most of what Stewart had to say. He divided us into groups of four or five and had us list ideas that would make us feel or play better. "We need better security in the parking lot," Danny Clay joked.

"We need better food after games," Jose Castro said. "I think we should fire Wild Bill."

Then Stewart rolled out the worst cliché of all. "*You're only a phone call away from Montreal,*" he said. He asked us what we thought it would take us, as individuals, to get there.

"An earthquake," Horse said.

"A plane crash," someone else chimed in.

We lost again, 3–2. At the beginning of the season, players would hang around the clubhouse after games and unwind for a while. Now it's a race to the showers. Nobody wants to stay in such a depressing atmosphere. Guys still take grounders, show up for extra hitting and all the other normal activities, but once the game starts it feels like we're playing not to win but to avoid losing.

Monday, May 21
Indianapolis

Rochester shut us out this afternoon, 3-0, finishing off a three-game sweep of us, the defending-champion Indians. Chris Marchok pitched two scoreless innings of relief, probably the two most important innings of his career. He was summoned by manager Tim Johnson and Joe a few days ago for a private evaluation of his work thus far. Harvard Head was told he wasn't making the grade.

"I'm afraid to put you in any games," Tim said. "I only do it on Joe's insistence. It's up to me whether you stay here or go back to Double-A, so shit or get off the pot."

Chris took it as an ultimatum, and today I guess you could say he earned the right to stay on the pot. Chris only has fourteen innings of work for the season, and he could complain about not being used enough to stay sharp, but that's an excuse that management never wants to hear. In addition, Chris knows we have eight relievers, instead of the normal five. A pitcher in Chris's situation is told that, if he really is mentally tough, he'll wait for his opportunity and capitalize on it. These same people, of course, will find a hundred ways to justify poor outing after poor outing from a highly touted prospect.

In 1983, I spent a month with the San Diego Padres and got only five innings of work. The same held true the following year when I was called up to the Phillies. The White Sox gave me a whopping seven innings in the month I spent with them in 1985. I was up with Seattle most of the year in 1986 and pitched just twenty-one innings. I'd always been a starter in Triple-A, and yet, in all those years, I only had one start.

I don't think relief pitchers who are used sparingly are as out of touch with mental toughness as old-school management is with reality.

Tuesday, May 22
Indianapolis

Syracuse rolled into town tonight for a three-game series. Before we face any team, Joe has a meeting with all the players to go over the opposing hitters. We determine how we'll pitch each batter and how we'll position ourselves in the field. Today, when Joe was finished, Tim stepped forward. "We all take this game too serious sometimes," he said. "We treat it as though it's a matter of life or death. We put too much pressure on ourselves and then if we strike out with men on base as a hitter or don't get that crucial out as a pitcher, we think the world's coming to an end. This isn't pressure. Pressure was in Vietnam, where my life depended on the man next to me. Baseball's not as important as we make it out to be. What's important is going home afterward to your wife and family, knowing they're healthy and they love you. Your family should always come first, then baseball. This is just a game, and it's the greatest game in the world, so have fun playing it. If we can't have fun, what's the sense of being here?"

It was exactly what we needed to hear. The dugout was more lively tonight, we were fundamentally sound, Scott pitched outstanding baseball, and we won 4–2. After the game, the stereo was blasting and guys were laughing for a change. Castro and Wild Bill were threatening each other again.

For the most part, speeches are overrated. The best managers, like Tony LaRussa, are those who don't overestimate their impact on a team. Tim's speech worked because it focused on a proper perspective rather than burying us with the problems we already knew we had. It took a load off our backs instead of adding to it.

Wednesday, May 23
Indianapolis

Randy Braun and Jose Castro were released today. They're both close friends of mine. Randy's thirty and Jose's thirty-two. The only guys older than them are Horse, who's thirty-four; Dwight Lowry, thirty-two; and me. I'm two weeks away from thirty-three.

We all knew moves had to be made to accommodate players coming off the disabled list. "I'd be foolish," Randy told me yesterday, "not to think I could be one of the people they let go." So Randy's not foolish, but he's also not a ballplayer anymore. Tim told him he has a beautiful family (which he does) and a good job to go back to, so it won't be as difficult for him to get on with his life. That may be true, but as Randy said tonight, "I wouldn't have left my accounting firm and family for six weeks of spring training with no pay if this wasn't what I wanted to do. I understand it, though. That's baseball." Randy's a class act. The team's collective IQ was dealt a severe blow with his departure.

Jose and I had played together with the White Sox, Blue Jays, and Royals before coming here. "Nachi" and I have been through a lot together. He was given the option to coach in West Palm Beach for the Expos' Rookie League team. "I've played this game for fourteen years," he said. "I always knew someday it'd be over. I guess that's today." He isn't sure what he's going to do yet. Like Randy, Jose has two children.

Unlike the other older guys here—Horse, Costello, Dwight Lowry, German Rivera and me—neither Randy or Jose ever spent a day in the major leagues. I don't write that out of pity. They wouldn't want your sympathy. They enjoyed the game and did the best they could.

We won 5–4 tonight. I had a mediocre outing and didn't figure in the decision. I took a bullet off my shin, and Tim relieved me. I was pretty hot, at least until I made my way up to the clubhouse. I watched Randy and Jose packing up, and my problems seemed kind of petty. I didn't figure in that decision, either. The decisions they face are the real-world variety, where things are more complicated than winning and losing.

Thursday, May 24
Indianapolis

John Costello was called back up to Montreal today. John pitched in relief yesterday and was evidently deemed healthy enough to return. John threw fairly well; I have no beef with him going to the big leagues.

I came out of last night's game with the lead. It stood until Syracuse scored off John in the ninth. Horse came on in relief of John and, when we scored in the bottom of the ninth, picked up the win.

First of all, I was charged with three runs myself, so I'm in no position to throw stones at another's performance. Plus the fact that John surrendered a run only proves he's human. Still, it's hard to see a guy who lost a win for you go up to the big leagues the very next day.

There is a misconception among many baseball followers who believe the quality of play between the various classifications of pro ball is enormous. Some fans think a big league pitcher would go undefeated in Triple-A or that Tony Gwynn would hit .800 against a Double-A pitcher. While it's true that the best players are almost always found in the majors, there's not nearly the separation of talent one might assume. Big leaguers are not the gods that the media, or the players themselves, make them out to be. By the same token minor leaguers aren't piss ants.

Already this year, I've squared off against two starters who are now in the big leagues, Shawn Boskie and Danny Jackson. I didn't get a decision in the first game and recorded a win in the second. They're both pitching well up there, too. I see no reason why I couldn't hold my own also.

Friday, May 25
Pawtucket

We arrived at our hotel at four. We had an hour to change clothes and eat before the bus left for the park. Today was my day to throw on the side. Joe Kerrigan suggested that I not worry too much about anything other than loosening my body up and letting the blood flow through my arm. Everyone's pretty washed out on any travel day, especially today, after being rain-delayed until midnight the night before.

I felt fine afterward and asked Joe if he'd help me with another pitch, maybe a curveball. This will probably be my last year unless I get back up, and I have nothing to lose by adding something else. He was in favor of the idea. Joe enjoys teaching and I like to learn, so if nothing else it'll be fun.

We won 5–3 in ten innings. That's acceptable, but the game had the makings of a dream come true. It was a normal game until the eighth inning. At that time, our hitting instructor, Gomer Hodge, approached me. "Fire," he whispered. "You might want to go in and put your spikes on, 'cause we're out of extra players." I was gone and returned in minutes with my glove packed inside my jacket.

I knew it was a long shot, but I was prepared. I felt like Barney Fife, gun in my holster, bullet in my pocket, out of harm's way. Then, in the tenth, James Steels twisted his ankle rounding third. I pulled out my glove and pounded my fist in the pocket. As luck would have it, the injury wasn't serious enough to keep James out of the lineup. I was always the pinch runner last year in Omaha, but I never made a defensive appearance. I can take some comfort in knowing I'm the man Gomer will come to, I guess.

In an effort to solidify their selection, I asked Tim after the game what batting group I should hit with tomorrow.

He laughed me out of his office.

Saturday, May 26
Pawtucket

Bob Malloy came up from Double-A a couple weeks ago and has been pitching well in relief. He got in last night's game and struck out the side in his inning of work. According to Chris Marchok, his roommate, Bob spent most of the night awake, pumped up and bouncing off the walls. A lot of players, especially pitchers, take hours to unwind after games, whether they're on a high produced by a strong outing, or they're fighting depression caused by getting ripped around the park. Bob is understandably fired up about what's happening with his career.

I remember my first year in Triple-A, in Hawaii. I had annually climbed the Padre ladder, was pitching as well as anybody in the league, and to top it off, had married Patty at midseason—over in Hawaii, of all romantic places. Back then, after a good night on the mound, I'd get back to the apartment, armed with a case of beer, and sit down at the kitchen table to figure up my ERA. Patty and I thought we had everything going for us, and we celebrated accordingly. All we really had was a black-and-white perspective on a predominantly gray situation.

Sometimes I miss those days, though, even if we were wrong in our expectations. The excitement of being one step (just a phone call) away was real. We still believed that good statistics would earn me a promotion, so Patty and I got more and more pumped up as starts continued to bring wins. I was making a cool $1,400 a month, which more than met our vagabond, childless needs. I'd see other players in their thirties and think, *no way you'll ever catch me here when I'm that old.*

It was fun. It was simple. It was simple-minded. I wish I could still feel that enthusiasm after games. I enjoy playing the game, and losing still grinds my teeth, but winning or pitching well doesn't do as much for me as it used to. I don't have any trouble getting to sleep after big games anymore.

Sunday, May 27
Pawtucket

There was good news and bad news today. Horse was called up to Montreal. John Costello blew his arm out and they're in need of a reliever. There was really no doubt about who deserved to go. Horse has the experience and has been our most consistent reliever by far. He's also the type of guy who's easy to pull for, so that makes it all even better.

Of course, now I'm the oldest guy on the team.

Mel Rojas, now fully recovered from the chicken pox, came off the disabled list today. Somebody had to go, and it was Danny Clay. They released him. Danny was a manager's dream. He had a great attitude, worked his butt off, and kept his mouth shut. A week ago, at the coaching staff's request, Danny switched to a sidearm delivery. He'd struggled a little, but mostly his release was a result of a numbers crunch.

Joe Kerrigan had a meeting with pitchers before tonight's game. From now on, each walk will cost the pitcher who issued it a dollar. Two bucks if the guy eventually scores. It won't hurt me much, but some guys here are going to be taking a pretty hefty pay cut. Yesterday, Pawtucket's first four runs each got on base via a walk. Tonight we won 12–3. One walk.

As I write this, I'm on a bus from Pawtucket to Scranton. We left about ten-thirty, and we should get to Scranton at about four. We bitch about this stuff, but no one's holding a gun to our heads, demanding we play baseball. I'd wager that a lot of people wouldn't mind playing baseball for a living, even if an occasional bus ride were included in the package.

Monday, May 28
Scranton

We won tonight, 8–7. Of the fifteen runs scored, two were earned. Both teams booted the ball all over the park. It's an artificial-turf surface, so bad hops weren't to blame. Howard Kellman, our radio announcer, told me after the game that we haven't played an errorless game for three weeks. That's unheard of. A decent college team doesn't go that long without an error-free game. Scott said that, because of the miscues, I threw twenty to thirty additional pitches tonight. However, just because I should have already been out of the inning doesn't give me license to serve up a three-run bomb. The hitter, Steve Stanicek, obviously disagreed. As sloppy as the game was, I came away with a win and no earned runs. I walked two and struck out four.

I saw baseball "analyst" Peter Gammons again tonight. He was theorizing (as only an analyst can) how Montreal's starting pitching is now by far the best in their division. He seemed to have conveniently forgotten his earlier report that the Expos staff would need help soon and that, if Montreal is to compete, Howard Farmer would "have" to be coming up in May. May is history. Howard's still with us. Montreal's competing.

One of the luxuries of being a baseball expert, I guess, is that you can change your colors and few will ever notice. Or is it possible that few really care what you say in the first place? Baseball is a highly unpredictable game, played by highly unpredictable men. How's that for an analysis?

Tuesday, May 29
Scranton

I spoke with my agents, Bob Gilhooley and Jim Bronner, today. They shared a rather interesting story with me during the course of our conversation. The Cubs have been looking to strengthen their bullpen since spring training, and one of general manager Jim Frey's options was Doug Bair. Doug is an experienced righthander with a good fastball and a hard curve. He's also forty years old.

Frey had little doubt that Doug could help the Cubs, but there's always that chance it might not work out. If that happened, the media in Chicago would go nuts. That was a chance Frey wouldn't take. He'd be subject to far less criticism if he brought up some homegrown kid who's clearly not ready than he would if he brought up some useful but older reliever.

Tonight's game has been canceled due to rain. Praise be. I'll read a while, go get something to eat, and then probably catch some of whatever baseball game that's televised. I doubt there are too many people who enjoy their job enough to watch others do it. I probably complain too much, but I do appreciate this game. I've seen its down sides, and as a result, some of the excitement has passed, but baseball will always be a part of me.

I called Patty and the boys tonight, as I do almost every night. They're all fine, which is music to my ears. Our new baby is due in just six weeks. I guess you don't ever *get* an old baby, do you? That's what your other kids become. I hope they handle it well, especially Sammy, who's been the new baby for five years.

Wednesday, May 30
Scranton

Howard shone tonight. His troubles had continued through his previous two starts, but he enjoyed perhaps his finest outing tonight. Six innings, two runs, three hits, one walk, seven strikeouts—and a loss. Montreal's not too concerned with his wins and losses, though. They just want to see some quality starts strung together. The wins will come anyway, if he deals the ball like he did tonight.

I think Howard's difficulties this season might stem from his disappointment at not making the Expos' pitching staff this spring. If that's the case, I can relate. Following the '83 season with the Padres, I was traded to the Phillies. I was overjoyed to part company with San Diego and Dick Williams. As a result, I worked hard over the winter to make a good impression on my new team. I went to spring training in Clearwater, Florida, determined to throw the cover off the ball. I had a brilliant spring, and it was obvious the Phillies liked their new acquisition. The last day of spring camp, they took the team picture, to be printed in the program in Philly. I was in it.

We concluded the exhibition season with the Pirates and I

remember Ruppert Jones, a teammate of mine in San Diego, congratulating me on making the Phillies.

That night, on the eve of the team flight out of Florida, they cut me. There had been a trade that had fallen through, a trade which would have unloaded a veteran pitcher and created a roster spot for me. I was crushed.

It wasn't as though I thought, "I'm bitter and I have nothing to prove in Triple-A, so I'll spend this season sulking." But I did sulk. I let circumstances beyond my control ruin my attitude. The more people told me I belonged in Philadelphia, the more I believed them—and the worse I pitched. I was oblivious to the cycle I created, but the Phillies noticed. It took me three months of getting slapped around the park in Portland, Oregon, to wake up and realize it had been *their* decision to cut me, but it was *mine* to do nothing about it.

It happens though, and not just in baseball. I wasn't the charter member of the "Poor Me" fraternity, and I wasn't its last inductee. It's possible that Howard is more focused on where he feels he *ought* to be instead of where he *is*. If so, we all hope he doesn't waste a year figuring it out. Years have a way of adding up.

Thursday, May 31
Indianapolis

I looked at the league statistics today when I got to the clubhouse. I'm still leading the league in innings pitched (with seventy) and my ERA (2.57) is third. I'm 4–4, but wins don't consume me as they did in years past. In high school and college, I hardly knew what an ERA was. I didn't care if the score was 25–24, just so we won. When my high school team won the Ohio state championship, nobody cared who did what. No one had to preach the importance of unity and enthusiasm. And college was much the same.

Now, if I win a game but give up a ton of runs in the process,

I'm more than a little upset. It's still the same game, but it's not an extracurricular activity anymore. It'll always be a team sport, but, professionally, once your livelihood depends on it, it's also an individual sport.

There are loads of players—guys who might have flunked math in high school—who can calculate their batting average or ERA after each at-bat or inning-pitched, before they even get to the dugout. It's unavoidable. Guys don't stay in baseball because they happened to be on a winning team the year before. They stay because of their individual accomplishments.

I couldn't believe how much fun I had playing softball the summer of '87. It was fun because if I made an out, no one, including me, got particularly upset. It was a game again.

There's a popular coaching phrase, "There's no 'I' in 'team.' " Compare Will Clark's contract with some utility infielder's before you buy into that cliché.

June

Friday, June 1
Indianapolis

After batting practice, Tim held a short meeting, just to remind us that the season is in full stride. "It's June now, fellas," he said, "and we all know where we're at."

True. In last place, nine games behind Buffalo.

"We've dug ourselves a hole," he said, "and nobody can get us out of it except the people sitting in this room. We're all in this shit. We're either going to go down together or come out of it together. Our first priority should be to get back to .500. When we meet that, we'll go from there. I haven't given up on you guys and I sure hope you haven't either. That's all I've got."

The radio and TV went back on, guys continued playing cards or doing crossword puzzles, others picked up their magazines and read—or looked, depending on the magazine. It wasn't that nobody heard what Tim had to say. After you've played for a while you understand that slapping each other on the back an hour before the game or cultivating an intense hatred for the other team doesn't necessarily produce success. We all know, or should know, what it takes for us as individuals to get ready. All Tim wanted to do was point out that it's not as early as we may think, and if we're going to make a move, now might be a nice time.

Patty and the boys are coming down tomorrow. It's been two weeks since I've seen them. Whenever I get caught up in the idea of this being my last year, I wonder how many starts I have left in my career or just how many days remain in this season. I never get carried away with being too melancholy about it, though, because on that same final day, I'll no longer have to count the days I get to spend with my family. I look forward to getting a job, taking the garbage out on Wednesdays, and tripping over stray toys. I never thought I'd sound like Erma Bombeck, but I guess I do.

Saturday, June 2
Indianapolis

The game was delayed tonight due to tornado warnings and heavy rains. A twister actually touched down within the city around seven-thirty, which was game time. The rain stopped at one point, prompting the umpires to designate an eight-forty-five start. I stretched the arm out and warmed up to begin the game. As the National Anthem was being sung, the clouds dumped on us. I pitched one inning before the tarps were again placed over the field. They never came back off. I threw twelve pitches, and then Joe told me that I wouldn't start tomorrow's game. "You had twelve in the game, plus the fifty-five you had in the bullpen *before* the game. Even if this game resumes tonight, you're not pitching. You'll just miss a turn."

The weather doesn't fall under my jurisdiction; I had to accept it.

After the game was called, the boys escorted me into the clubhouse. That is nearly the equivalent of heaven to them. It boggles their minds to talk to the guys and drop subtle hints like, "How many gloves do you *have* in your locker?" or "I didn't know catchers needed *three* pairs of shin guards."

Don't laugh. It seems to work. At home, they've got a catcher's glove from Dave Valle, a hat from Pete Ladd, and shin guards from Joel Skinner. I talk to the boys often about this year possibly being my last. They say they want me to play forever. They don't realize how much of our family has been sacrificed for this career because, for the most part, it's all they've ever known. They have no idea how hard it is on Patty. For that matter, I probably don't either.

Sunday, June 3
Indianapolis

I had an interesting chat with Howard today at the park. I don't think he wanted any advice as much as he needed an ear to talk to.

"I can't *believe* the season is only two months old," he said. "I feel like it's August instead of June. I worked hard all winter to get here. Now that I'm here I wish I was back home. I don't feel that way all the time. Some days I look forward to coming here, but other days I hate it. You ever feel that way?"

The first thought that came to my mind was that this guy is having a rather dismal year thus far and isn't living up to expectations, Montreal's or his own. I doubt he'd wish he was home if he was tearing up the league. I didn't tell him that, of course. I didn't tell him, either, that my attitude is able to remain somewhat consistent through the bad times largely because I've been separated from the game. I doubt he'd know what I meant.

"I've had what you want," I said, "and that helps to keep me from feeling like you feel now."

If I let myself, I can think of dozens of things I don't like about baseball. Being separated from my family sits way atop the list and will be the strongest consideration against continuing at the end of the year. Lord knows I have as many sob stories as the next guy when it comes to how I've been screwed.

But I've been removed from baseball before, in '87, at a time when I felt I was in my prime.

No matter how fortunate or unfortunate in his case a person feels, there's nothing like absence to increase appreciation. I was lucky because I was given another chance. Most aren't so lucky. The dreams of stardom, the money and the security that this game offers all disappeared that summer. Since baseball was no longer in my grasp, I thought of my situation as bad, period. I complain from time to time now, but underneath all that, I appreciate the goodness of this game.

Monday, June 4
Indianapolis

Joey, Sammy, and I went to the park a couple hours early this afternoon. We put on our uniforms and romped around the field in a happy and vigorous cycle of ground balls, hitting, and pitching. I figured it would wear them out, too, which would make Patty's drive home a lot easier.

When Patty appeared inside the stadium to pick them up, and I saw their expressions change, it hit me that this game triggers basically the same emotions in the boys as it does in me. They have fun playing outside and testing their bodies, often trying to do more than they're capable of. They like goofing around with the guys and engaging in verbal warfare, although they're still easy prey. They love the freedom and openness the park offers, too. But they feel the flip side. They're no good at saying good-bye. They're not fond of all the travel, and they've grown tired of figuring out how many more days until we're together again.

Howard pitched better and picked up a win, but he remains disgusted and sounded the same as usual after the game. "I never walk people like this," he'll lament, then he'll check his velocity. "Last year I threw ninety-four," he'll say, shaking his head.

He's also unhappy with his arsenal of pitches. "Last year I used my change-up all the time, no matter what the count was."

I wish I could throw ninety-two and be upset by it.

There's a feeling around here that Howard may be coming out of his slump. We need him, although if he throws well, we won't have him very long. Peter Gammons is one hundred percent correct in his judgment of Howard's ability. I just have a problem with presuming results.

Tuesday, June 5
Bryan, Ohio

I drove home today and spent the off day in Bryan. Patty had arranged Sammy's dental and her doctor's appointments so I could accompany them to the medical center. Dr. Dave Roebuck passed by while we were in the waiting area for Patty. Dave's son, Joe, was drafted two years ago by the Milwaukee Brewers out of high school. Joe was the stud athlete of Williams County. He was all-state in football and baseball and lettered three years in basketball. He had planned on attending the University of Michigan on a baseball scholarship before he was drafted.

But now, at the ripe age of twenty-one, Joe Roebuck is nearly fed up with baseball. He spent two seasons in rookie ball and has twice been invited by the Brewers to instructional league —a great sign for young players. Joe's future, though, has come to a standstill with the Brewers organization this year. He was not assigned to a team out of spring training and was kept in Arizona for what's called "extended spring"—epitome of limbo.

"He doesn't trust anyone anymore," Dave said. "They tell him how good he's doing, yet they won't do anything with him. All he wants is a chance to fail. If they'd send him to A ball and he didn't work out, he could live with that. At least he'd know.

He feels like he can still play, but he's getting tired of trying to prove it in Arizona."

Here's a twenty-one-year-old kid who feels he can "still" play. Most of us think of players pushing forty using that terminology. I've kept up with Joe as much as possible and I know it's been a rough road for him. Although he no doubt remains the envy of many young men in Bryan, his self-esteem has probably been hit pretty hard. In two years he's gone from loving baseball to being calloused to it.

Wednesday, June 6
Denver

I was one tired man today. I returned to Indy late last night and got up this morning at four to get to the park by five to catch the bus for our six-thirty flight to Denver. For some crazy reason, a twelve-thirty game was scheduled for this afternoon. We were feeling sorry for ourselves until we heard Denver had played a doubleheader in Toledo the night before—and both games had gone into extra innings. Then it was announced that the game would be delayed because the Denver team was stuck in Chicago waiting for their plane. The game finally started around two. Both teams were exhausted but put on a good show in spite of it. We won 5–2.

We've now won ten of our last fourteen games and have climbed to six games behind Buffalo. Nobody's talking championship just yet. We've all witnessed our potential for stinking it up too much to get cocky. For the first extended period this year, though, we're healthy. The injuries and chicken pox are gone, at least temporarily.

My boys called me tonight. Joey fell apart last night as I was leaving home. Patty said he cried himself to sleep holding a picture of me. I don't mention that to illustrate what a great father I must be for them to miss me so much. It makes me sick to know there's such a void in my sons' lives. When I said a couple days ago that I'm not above complaining, this is what I'm talking about.

The hurt and the disappointments of the game itself don't even compare to what I feel when Patty tells me stories like tonight. I appreciate what I have, yet I hate what it does at times. If that sounds contradictory, then you've grasped the struggle so many of us experience here.

Today was my birthday. Scott was the only one here who knew, and he knew only because Patty told him. Scott didn't make a big deal out of it, because he knew I wouldn't want him to. I observed my birthday with my family yesterday in Bryan. Patty brought me shrimp cocktail from the restaurant, and the boys got me a couple of New Kids on the Block tapes, which I "conveniently" left behind for them.

I'm thirty-three. At this point, birthdays aren't as dire as they were for me five or six years ago. Thirty-two, thirty-three, forty-three; what's the difference? Any way you look at it, I'm a fossil in my present environment.

Thursday, June 7
Denver

The man here who's had the biggest impact on our team's current winning ways is our catcher, Gil Reyes. His insertion in the lineup coincided exactly with our better play—and that's been no coincidence.

Gil was on the disabled list early in the year, and we had another catcher, Jerry Goff, who was considered a prospect. When Jerry was called up, Nelson Santovenia was sent down and—as you might imagine—was put behind the plate nearly every day. Nellie was recalled a couple weeks ago and the pitchers here were ecstatic. We were happy for both Jerry and Nellie, but, selfishly, we were delighted because we knew we'd have Gil catching us.

Gil is the leader of this team on the field and in the club-house. That is a fact. He is also demented. That is undisputed. He leads by energy, enthusiasm, and volume. He's bilingual, too, so nobody's shortchanged.

Case in point. Gil and Joe Kerrigan work well together as far as how to attack opposing hitters. Gil called a slider to-night with two strikes on a hitter who Joe thought we should just bury with fastballs inside. They started pulling each other's chain, Joe from the dugout and Gil from behind the plate.

"Gil!" Joe yelled. Gil ignored him. "Gil!"

Gil looked at the dugout. "Shut up!"

Joe couldn't believe it, but you could tell he was enjoying the verbal battle with Gil. "What are you *doing*?"

Gil started laughing at Joe and waved his glove at him as if to say "buzz off."

"Listen to your pitching coach," Joe said.

"Shut up."

The next pitch was a fastball inside for a weak ground ball and the third out. Gil returned to the dugout and the shouting match resumed, this time face-to-face.

"That's a wasted pitch on him," Joe said. "What are you thinking?"

"He's sittin' on the fastball," Gil said. "I wanted to give him something else to think about, then come back in and bust him."

"That's stupid," Joe said. "That's just a wasted pitch."

"You're stupid."

Then Joe dropped the hammer on him. "Listen, Gil. It's like when *you're* hitting. Why would anyone want to waste a slider on *you*?"

They both cracked up and Gil walked to the opposite end of the dugout, utilizing his Spanish to abuse Joe. Mutual respect shows itself in strange ways sometimes.

In fairness to Gil, I should add that he has a hose for an arm. In the two games here, he's thrown out all three runners attempting to steal and picked another off second base. It's closer to expected than surprising. He's as good a catcher as I've ever had, minor or major league.

Friday, June 8
Denver

Our five-game winning streak is over. I saw to it. We lost 5–1; I went six innings and gave up four runs. Our defense was shaky at times and two of the runs that scored came in on errors. I'm not pointing fingers, though. I sucked. I had absolutely no location. I gave up *twelve* hits, one walk, and struck out four. Most of their hits were ground balls that got through the infield, though there were a couple legitimate hits. Easily legitimate. There was one that cleared the left-field wall and kept rising. There was also that line drive that hit me an inch above my left kneecap. They replayed it on the Diamond Vision. I didn't watch, but it must have been brutal, judging from the groans from the fans. It hurt, but I was far too masculine to admit even a limp. Now that I'm tucked away in my hotel room, I'll confess that I can hardly walk. One inch down and I'd have been history. Joe came up to me after the sixth to tell me I was finished. "That's it, Fire," he said. "You battled your tits off."

I've been told that many times before and I guess I'll accept the compliment, but it frustrates me to no end. "If I was *that* good," I told Scott, "I wouldn't have to battle like I do. It's not like I crave men on base so I can show how well I can fight to get out of a jam."

I get complimented as a battler all the time because I'm often in positions where my back's to the wall. It's not by design, but it sure must appear that way. Tonight's effort will be better off forgotten. I'll only remember it when I move my leg.

Saturday, June 9
Oklahoma City

Joe Kerrigan joined me at breakfast this morning. He wasn't in his seat ten seconds before he said, "Fire, we're gonna change you. The new delivery isn't adding velocity like we'd hoped. All it's doing is taking away from your location."

Last night probably had something to do with that deduction.

"First van to the park is at four," he said. "Be on it, and I'll show you what we're gonna do." I got on it and he showed me. The new windup feels strange, but Joe's convinced it'll keep the ball down more consistently. We'll see.

John Costello came down for the day from Montreal. He's on the disabled list again, although he claims there's no injury. He was told to come here, throw two innings, and then report back to the Expos tomorrow. We had a 1–0 lead going into the seventh inning tonight, whereupon it became John's time to "get his work in."

Oklahoma City scored to tie it up in the bottom of the seventh. John went out in the eighth and walked the first two hitters he faced on ten pitches, at which point Tim removed him from the game.

Jim Davins came in and pitched well, allowing only the man on second to score. Romy Cucjen hit a two-run dinger in the ninth and Jim preserved our lead for a 3–2 victory.

I was in the stands doing the pitching chart with the radar gun. John threw thirty-six pitches in one official inning of work: twenty balls, sixteen strikes. He threw six sliders, all for balls. The rest were fastballs. Fastballs in the mid-80's. He struck out two and walked three.

Here's the punch line: his bags are packed and he's off to the big leagues. No one's laughing.

Losing Costello to Montreal has actually made us a much better team. Ask any player here. That isn't usually the case, obviously, but it's worked out that way.

As I mentioned earlier, nobody here has anything against

John. It's the politics of baseball. He's probably experienced the underside of it, too, at some point in his career.

After Davins bailed Costello out, he looked at John's pitching chart. "Oh, *now* I get it," Jim said, slapping his forehead. "*Now* I know what I have to do to get up there."

Sunday, June 10
Oklahoma City

Chris Marchok hasn't pitched in about a week (again), and he apparently passed this information on to a friend of his on Oklahoma City's team. Chris was sitting on the bullpen bench, beside Joe Kerrigan, as Howard began warming up for this afternoon's game. As Chris's friend passed our bullpen on the way to their dugout, he thought he'd be cordial and say hi to Chris. "Hey, Chris," the guys says, obviously with sarcasm. "Good luck just in case you happen to get into the game for a third of an inning or something."

That's not what you want a "friend" to say when you're prac-tically sitting on your pitching coach's lap. Joe has a whole lot of influence concerning who gets used and who doesn't. Chris just buried his head. He didn't even look at Joe.

"I didn't know," Chris told me later, "whether to laugh or cry."

The weakness that has remained even through our recent wins is our defense. It caught up with us today. We had seven runs after the first two innings and lost 10–9. We committed four errors and let all kinds of runs in. Tim wasn't impressed. "We played like we were waiting to lose all day," he said. "That's the worst exhibition of baseball I've ever seen in my life! That's horseshit."

It truly was.

I called home tonight. Patty is only one month away from her due date and is rapidly running out of energy. Both boys are out of school for the summer, which is great unless you're eight months pregnant and have to keep an eye on them.

She told me something tonight I thought I'd hear five years ago. "For the first time in my life," she said, "just for a little while tonight, I wished you weren't playing baseball."

We talked about how there's only a few months left. Somehow that seemed more appropriate than telling her about the new windup I started tinkering with today.

Monday, June 11
Oklahoma City

There were more moves today. Lefthanded reliever Steve Frey came down on rehabilitation. What they'll do when Steve's arm is given a clean bill of health is anybody's guess.

Chris Nabholz, from Double-A Jacksonville, was called up to Montreal to pitch a game of a doubleheader. More than likely he'll be returned to Double-A after his start, but I wouldn't bet the house on it. He's having a great year, 7–2 with a 3.03 ERA. Scott is 6–3 here with a 2.90 ERA and has been our best starter the past couple weeks. My ERA is 2.61, but I've thrown poorly lately; it'd be ridiculous for me to feel slighted.

Montreal went to a prospect for help in this situation. Which they should. Why get a glimpse of someone you have no plans for when the opportunity presents itself to take a peek at a kid who may spend ten years in your big league rotation? I'd do the same thing if I were them.

The point is that major league clubs don't automatically take their hottest Triple-A pitcher. Scott understands how it works. Besides, Nabholz is lefthanded and the Expos are facing the Phillies, who have trouble with lefties.

Jim Davins—the same guy who two days ago bailed out Costello (who's now struggling up in the big leagues)—was sent to Double-A today. Jacksonville's in first place and supposedly needs a closer. The front office is telling Jim much more than the transaction will read, and he knows it. What he hears is that he's not in the Expos' future, not that he ever thought he was. They're asking him to bolster the organization by helping Jacksonville win the Southern League. That'd be a feather in the Expos' cap, but what's Jim have to gain?

The optimist will say that he ought to go down there, save every game he can, and everything will come out okay. I'm close enough with Jim to know he'll do his best to arrive at and maintain that attitude. He sure tried to while he was here.

Tuesday, June 12
Indianapolis

In response to the Davins move, Joe had a brief meeting with the pitchers. "There are a lot of things that happen in this game that are out of our control," Joe said. "You guys should know that by now. Two relievers in Jacksonville have blown their arms out and the organization feels it's important that they win there in order to keep a solid working relationship. I just want you to know that neither Tim nor I had anything to do with this and it certainly doesn't reflect what we think Jim can do on the mound. It was out of our control."

Joe wasn't trying to pass the buck or sugar-coat the situation. He's taken credit for unpopular decisions before. He just communicated honestly about a matter he knew bothered us. The pitchers here aren't on a search-and-destroy mission. We don't feel the need to find out who's responsible so we can lynch the guy. This stuff happens, all the time, and we do, as Joe said, know that by now.

An "old school" coach or manager would never have addressed the issue, though, much less hinted at any form of compassion. That wouldn't be in keeping with the macho standards they've lived (and died) with. It's called communication, and "men" respond to it. This game will be better off when the few dinosaurs still in the game are extinct.

Tim had a meeting of his own with the team. "Our defense

stinks," he said, "but I'm not going to put up with pitchers showing up our own players anymore. It's not as easy as you pitchers think. The next time I see it happening, I promise I'll do everything in my power to get you out of here." What he means is a pitcher who openly shows his displeasure toward a teammate after that particular player has booted a ball.

It was a speech designed not only to admonish Howard, whose frustrations have become ever more transparent, but also to warn the rest of us. After that, Tim and Howard had a closed-door meeting. That's communication, too, and it's every bit as necessary.

Wednesday, June 13
Indianapolis

After losing both games of a doubleheader yesterday, we bounced back with a win tonight. It was the first game with my latest delivery and Joe and I were both pleased with it. I can only recall three fly-ball outs in the six innings I pitched, and I struck out all of two hitters, so there were a lot of ground balls. I gave up six hits, two runs, and walked one.

I threw too many pitches, ninety-nine, as a result of taking too many hitters too deep into the count. I didn't throw as high a percentage of strikes as usual. I was missing low, or at least that's what the umpire thought. All the ground balls, coupled with the low calls that could have gone the other way, may indicate that the delivery's working.

We had a packed house tonight. It wasn't because I was on the mound either. Ted Giannoulas, the Famous Chicken, formerly the San Diego Chicken, entertained the fans during the game. Without exaggeration, I've pitched in seventy-five percent of the games he's been present at, with whatever team I've been with, whether we're at home or on the road. Back in May, when the scoreboard was flashing upcoming events and I saw that Ted was coming, I told Scott I'd be pitching June 13. He frowned. "How do you know that?"

I pointed to the scoreboard. "The Chicken's here June 13th," I said. "I always pitch for Ted."

Scott looked skeptical, but sure enough, I drew that start.

Ted finishes his act in the seventh inning, and it seems I've been done with mine after six lately, so the two of us sat in the clubhouse and recalled names and stories from the past. We go back to the early '80s together. I was dressed in underwear and ice while he sat adorned in his chicken outfit, minus the head.

We talked about autograph seekers, more specifically the rudeness of most of them. Ted gets mobbed, so he's more in tune than I am. Ted says he has five years left in him, easy. It's tough to judge the Chicken's longevity, though. There's a strong possibility he'll outlast me in this game.

Thursday, June 14
Indianapolis

The working hours in baseball often resemble that of a second-shift job. That makes for a lot of spare time during the day. Before I get out of bed, I say a prayer and read a while. Then I head straight for the coffeemaker and brew a few cups for the morning. I make myself some breakfast and usually turn the tube to CNN to stay in touch with what's going on in the world—unless of course it's Saturday, in which case I look for Looney Tunes.

I'll look over the morning paper (all sections) until I'm convinced my breakfast has settled. I then do my morning workout—one hundred to one hundred and fifty sit-ups and fifty to seventy-five push-ups in various positions. It's very loosely based on Steve Carlton's warm-up, which I learned when I was with the Phillies in '84.

After the workout, I shower and run errands, then return to the apartment and touch up or overhaul what I've written in this journal the previous day.

Then I make lunch. I can only recall eating out twice in Indy, even when Patty and the boys are here. I'm by no means a gourmet chef, but I make sure I get veggies and fruit. I'll do the dishes, clean the apartment, and pop in my contacts.

I like to get to the park early so I can run on my own. If that sounds like it's written in the spirit of a distance runner, you're misled. It's actually quite the opposite. My motive behind arriving early, at home as well as on the road, is that it allows me to run outside the confines of the stadiums. I'll run on the streets, my headphones clamped to my ears. The music takes my mind off how much I hate running. Rick Williams uses the same method.

After four or five miles, I come back, shower, and get dressed for batting practice. I like to "power shag" whenever possible, which involves patrolling center field and going after anything I can get a glove on. After batting practice, I go in the clubhouse, do my weights, and heckle people. I sit through the game, either in the stands or the dugout.

I go back to the apartment afterward and, if it's not too late, I call Patty, but that's not even always possible because it's an hour later in Ohio than Indiana. I fix something to eat, read a while, say a prayer, and go to bed, usually between midnight and 1 A.M.

Friday, June 15
Indianapolis

The slim chance I have of returning to the big leagues was greatly diminished today. I arrived at the park ready to throw on the side and was instead asked by Joe to join him in Tim's office. I could tell by the expression on his face it wasn't good news.

"Fire, something's come up," Joe said. "I should probably wait on Tim so we could tell you together, but I'm not going to. I don't want you to walk out on the field and learn about it that way. Montreal has sent Nabholz here and they want him in the rotation. We've talked it over and you're the logical choice to make room for him. We've got four prospects now in the rotation and you know as well as I do we can't touch them. John Boles, Rick Williams, Tim, and I discussed it and we felt that, between you and Andy [Scott Anderson], you'd be better suited for the pen. This has absolutely nothing to do with your work habits either. They're great. It'd be easy for me to sit here and tell an asshole this. We like the hell out of you. You know that. I just sent my reports in on our players and what I wrote about you was that if a couple pitchers went down up there you could help. I also said that your biggest asset to this organization would probably be as a pitching coach someday. I know this comes as a blow to you and I know how hard you work, but this is the way it's going to be. If a spot opens up, you'll be right back in there. Hopefully that's what'll happen."

All this was tough to hear, tougher to react to in a professional manner. I regrouped as best I could. "I know somewhere along the line, some older pitcher was probably bumped to make room for me when I was up-and-coming. I understand that I'm the logical choice, but *you* have to understand I'm better suited for starting."

"I know that," he acknowledged. We got up and I said I'd do the best I can. "I know that, too," he said.

I walked out of the office and the first person I came across was Chris Nabholz. He's a great kid, and I welcomed him to the team. Then I got my uniform on and wound my way through the stadium and out beyond the left-field grandstand. I stood there alone, and watched Chris warm up. I guess I felt sorry for myself for a little while, but I'm trying to fight it. The game is bigger than any individual. I've known that for a long time. Maybe I needed to be reminded.

Saturday, June 16
Indianapolis

Patty and the boys arrived yesterday for the weekend. She isn't exactly thrilled about my new role either, but she's seen this happen all too many times.

I grabbed a stat sheet before I left the park last night to submit as evidence. Not of a crime or any severe injustice, but to show how decisions are made at this level. As you can see I'm fifth in the league in ERA. I also rank third or fourth in innings pitched, and, had it not been for the suspended game I started, I'd probably lead the league in that department. Check out all those strikeouts, too!

PITCHING TOP 10 (MINIMUM 51 IP)

PITCHER	CLUB	W—L	ERA	IP	H	BB	SO
Hill, Ken	LOU	5—0	1.66	54	30	21	73
Scudder, Scott	NVL	5—1	2.18	58	40	23	49
Lopez, Rob	NVL	5—4	2.53	64	50	22	38
Taylor, Dorn	BUF	9—2	2.55	85	67	26	55
Fireovid, Steve	IND	5—5	2.63	82	91	19	30
Hammond, Chris	NVL	6—1	2.64	72	64	32	74
Brown, Keith	NVL	3—4	2.73	56	57	16	25
Blankenship, Kevin	IWA	6—1	2.77	55	55	27	39
Filson, Pete	OMA	10—2	2.93	80	84	21	49
Hinkle, Mike	LOU	5—2	2.96	52	50	10	23

Here also is a list of our other current starters in Indy:

	W—L	ERA	IP	H	BB	SO
Dan Gakeler	2—2	2.04	35	16	18	22
Scott Anderson	6—4	3.02	89	82	24	51
Mel Rojas	1—0	3.40	53	48	30	38
Howard Farmer	3—6	5.56	69	83	29	52

These figures aren't assembled to reflect how dominating I am. I'm not. Still, my numbers aren't embarrassing. There are other

considerations that don't show up here, such as age or experience, depending upon how you fit into the organization's
plans. A club may like an older player because of his experience,
yet be wary of another because of his age. It's a convenient
double-edged sword for them.

I'm not a product of this organization. I'm a journeyman
who's pitching here for the season. They've drafted and nur-
tured the others more than me. There's both money and time
invested in most prospects. I'm not saying that factors such
as these determine everyone's fate in the game. They do, however, constitute a large voice in what transpires. There's more
to professional baseball than statistics reveal. I don't consider
myself victimized by baseball. I just think the hill's a little
harder to climb for a man my age.

Sunday, June 17
Indianapolis

I've had my faults and shortcomings over the years in the game,
but the one thing I've rarely had to worry about has been my
attitude. It's not the best right now, although I expect it to
improve. As we said our good-byes this afternoon, I told Patty
I didn't even feel like going to the park today. That's pathetic.
How would you like a guy with that temperament coming out
of the pen with men on base?

Just because I understand the move doesn't mean I have to
like it. If Montreal feels Chris Nabholz can give them ten years
in the big leagues, that's great. That doesn't make my goals
any less meaningful to *me*. I think only a man with no soul
could wholeheartedly accept a career reversal based on cold
logic. In fact, if I were a coach, I'd be much more concerned if
a player responded to moves like this with a shrug of his shoulders. The situation doesn't give me permission to stomp my
feet or rant and rave, but I'm fully entitled to be upset with it.
What I hope, and I'm sure what Tim and Joe hope, is that I'll

channel the hostility I have in the one direction that's positive: toward the hitters.

My attitude was much better once I got to the park and ragged on a few guys, and I was ready to go by game time. I was the first man up in the second, third, and seventh innings, which gives me good reason to believe they plan on using me. The first time I got up I realized I'd forgotten my athletic supporter and cup. I'm used to wearing them once every five days.

My arm felt horrible afterward. My shoulder hurts, and, for the first time I can ever remember, my elbow aches. My left hand is bruised, too, where fellow reliever Eddie Dixon kicked it while warming up beside me. I'm not used to sharing the bullpen area.

Monday, June 18
Indianapolis

Chris Nabholz had his first start tonight. For two innings, he was perfect. "In six outs," I said to Davins, "he's got two strike-outs, two broken bats, and made a great defensive play. Hard to blame 'em for putting me in the pen." It'd be difficult to pull for him if he were a jerk, but that's not the case with Chris.

Chris was eventually charged with five runs in 4⅔ innings. Actually, he threw the ball pretty well throughout, but he made a couple of fat pitches at inopportune times. He's got good stuff. After Tim pulled him, I watched Chris walk from the mound, in control and unshaken. Guys who come out of the game with that kind of poise have *real* confidence, not the kind of angry, show-off confidence that tends merely to cover up for insecurity.

Jim Davins was returned to us today. The Double-A season is divided into halves and Jim was sent to be the closer during the final games of the first half. It never materialized. "We were blown out of the first three games I was there and eliminated."

He's still bitter about how the organization used him. "Ten-hour bus trips, eating at fast-food places, Double-A motels, no money, and wearing dirty clothes. I hated it."

He was sent down while we were on the road and joined them on a road trip, which accounts for the lack of money and the dirty clothes. "I bused with the team for ten hours from Birmingham back to Jacksonville," he said. "Then they tell me I'm going back to Indy. Why couldn't they have flown me out of Birmingham in the first place?"

He was exhausted tonight. He pitched two innings of relief for us and between them in the dugout he told me, "I could fall asleep right now, right here."

Chris Marchok was sent down to make room for Jim. Our roster doesn't remain the same for any length of time. That's not unique to this organization, though. As Jim and I were talking before the game in the clubhouse, he pointed into our trainer's office and asked me, "Who's that?"

"That's our new third baseman, Angel Salazar. We just got him."

Jim broke out laughing. "Right!"

"Really. He is!" I wasn't kidding.

"What's wrong with Romy?"

"Blew out his knee."

"Where'd we get this guy from?"

"Venezuela. He says he's twenty-eight."

Jim cracked up again, "I thought he was a scout." Jim shook his head. "Man, that's a *hard* twenty-eight."

Tuesday, June 19
Indianapolis

After batting practice today a few of us sat around and "got in the yearbook." That's a phrase for players talking about their accomplishments from the past. It's easy to overlook the athleticism that's assembled on a given team when all you see guys do is swing bats or throw balls. We have both a collegiate quarterback and goalie here, along with several others who had athletic opportunities outside baseball.

My background is probably typical. Growing up in Bryan, I played basketball and baseball in high school and was an all-state performer in both. I had offers from colleges to play both sports.

My heart was set on basketball, but my stature was better suited to baseball. Most colleges looked at me as a shortstop or third baseman. I was (still am if you can call it that) a switch-hitter and could handle the glove fairly well. I've always pitched, too, and during my senior year in high school, I tossed all our tournament games on the way to the state championship. I must emphasize that there was a ton of offensive talent on that team. I threw hard and I threw strikes and our bats did the rest.

I attended Miami University—the one in Ohio—on a baseball scholarship and played for Bud Middaugh. I put up good numbers there. Not great, but good. I was so naive about what baseball could provide. I was just having fun. Then one day during my sophomore year Bud called me into his office. He told me he had no doubt that I'd pitch in the major leagues someday. All I can remember thinking is "Wow. He means it!" That was the first time it occurred to me I could make a living with the ability I'd been given. I'll never forget that feeling. I walked out of his office on Cloud Ten. I didn't look at baseball as just a game anymore. From that day on I set my sights on a baseball career.

Looking back, I wish some administrator would have grabbed me by the neck and said, "Hey, stupid! You're going to spend a year and a half in the major leagues and ten or eleven in the minors. I have no doubts you'd make, say, a fine doctor."

Of course, I don't mean to suggest that anyone, other than me, should have been responsible for seeing that I got an education. And even if somebody *had* tried to shake some sense into me, I wouldn't have listened. What could be better than a career in baseball?

Wednesday, June 20
Indianapolis

My perspective on relieving has been improved, thanks to tonight's game. I made my first appearance, coming in with the bases loaded and two outs in the sixth. I'm not crazy about this particular predicament, I thought on my way to the mound, but there's no better way to see if I'm cut out for this type of work.

In classic fashion I worked the hitter to a full count. I'm sure the crowd of a couple thousand found it hard to contain themselves in all the excitement. Then, in typical fashion, the batter topped a slider for an infield hit. That was the only hit they got off me. I finished the game, going 3⅓ innings, and recorded the win. I walked two and fanned *five*. The five strikeouts tied my season high. It had been a week since I'd pitched, so I was a little rusty. That explains the two walks.

By the same token, my arm was well rested and I felt very strong. That explains the strikeouts. I hit 90 mph for the first time this year—or, for that matter, in several years. I threw three fastballs by a hitter who'd hit a four-hundred-foot shot in his previous at bat. They were in good spots, but nevertheless I haven't disposed of a hitter that way in ages. I came close to laughing out on the mound.

I've never consciously held anything back as a starter, but I'm thinking along the lines of nine innings—as opposed to two or three as a reliever. This "now or never" mind-set evidently improved my velocity. Tonight's outing was just what the doctor ordered.

Thursday, June 21
Bryan, Ohio

I drove home to Bryan last night after the game. We have the day off before leaving for a twelve-day, thirteen-game road trip. Sammy had tee-ball practice this morning and he'd have been crushed if Dad hadn't made it in time to watch him. Patty and the boys will accompany me to Columbus tomorrow and, during the following series against Toledo, I'll be able to stay at home. I'm the only one on the team who looks forward to Toledo.

Patty is big. She should be. She's just a few weeks away from her due date. I should clarify that. She's put on only seventeen pounds, but her belly is big. Her emotions cover a wide range these days. I do what I can, but too much of it's over the phone. Consequently, when I do have time with her, I often feel guilty. "I feel like you've missed so much of this baby's development," she says, by which she means that she feels sorry for me, not herself.

She's not begging for sympathy or trying to hurt me. It's a fact. It does hurt, though, and I do feel sorry for her. I know baseball isn't the only profession that separates husbands from expectant wives. I know it could be worse. What magnifies my uneasiness about the situation is that people might imagine that I'm flying around the country having the time of my life. Patty and I frequently come across people who think we live some sort of fairy-tale life because I throw baseballs for a living.

Their fascination with the game blinds them from any adverse side effects that might develop from it, which in this case happens to be a wife who could use more of her husband's help, and a husband who wishes he had more of it to offer. It's not self-centeredness that makes us feel this way. We don't want more attention. If anything, we've always wanted less. The most common phrase Patty hears from people is "It must be so exciting." Very few stop to realize it can be rough, at times, too. Sure it could be rougher, but by the same token it's not as grand as people might guess—and people *do* guess.

Friday, June 22
Columbus

It's impossible for a player to remain in baseball for any length of time without experiencing some embarrassment. I've had my share over the years, but there are a couple of incidents I'll always remember.

After a successful rookie-ball season, I was invited to the Padres' big league camp in '79. It was a chance for them to become familiarized with a recent draftee and also to receive a lot of batting practice. Looking back, the Padres' priorities were the latter first, the former second.

Anyway, I got to the clubhouse bright and early the first day of camp and strapped on my personalized uniform. Number 62. Not a good sign. We stretched and went through all the boring drills. It didn't bother me, though, because I thought I had arrived. I was a *San Diego Padre*.

Finally, it was my turn to throw on the side. I hustled to the bullpen and I realized that Gene Tenace was going to catch me. I *knew* I'd arrived then. I thought: Gene Tenace—this is the man who hit all those homers in the World Series! He was on those '70s Oakland teams that I thought were so cool because they wore white shoes and all had mustaches. I got to the mound, eager to show off my stuff.

Pitching coach Chuck Estrada was rubbing up a ball for me while I kicked the rubber. "Here ya go, kid," he said, tossing me the ball. I was so anxious to throw—so anxious to impress someone—that I caught it and, in the same motion, kicked my left leg up and fired the ball toward the plate. I looked up just as I was about to release the ball and saw Gene Tenace, looking down and putting on his glove. It's not in my best interests, I thought as I let go, to throw this ball. Too late. The ball was already in flight. From instinct maybe, Tenace looked up in time not only to see the ball coming but to catch it with his bare hand. He didn't say a word. He glowered at me, took a couple of steps in my direction, then fired a pea. I caught it out of self-preservation. My heart sunk. I'd have to make the team another day, I knew. I just wanted to get that day over with.

Saturday, June 23
Columbus

The one constant in baseball is change. Dan Gakeler hurt his elbow, and I was told today that I'll get his start in Toledo on Monday.

Sunday, June 24
Columbus

What a day! Columbus completed a three-game sweep of us. They never even had to use their bullpen. We're playing like we were earlier in the season, which is to say, pathetic. Even so, the team's woes had to take a backseat to what my family and I went through.

After the game, Patty and I loaded the boys in the car and headed for Bryan, where I'll stay while we play Toledo. Since it was a day game this afternoon, we'd planned on arriving home early enough to watch a movie together and, generally, just sit around and be a family.

But, a half-hour outside Columbus, the temperature gauge on our car began creeping upward. Mr. Goodwrench I'm not, but even *I* can recognize when a car is overheating. We pulled into a station, and I tended to the problem while the boys played catch and Patty read.

Forty-five minutes later we were back on the road. Ten minutes after that, we were at another gas station. It was now eight-fifty, and the station closed at nine. The attendant was pleasant but firm. "Can't possibly fix it tonight, folks." He did agree to take a peek at it, though. The boys resumed playing catch and Patty took up crying.

After exhausting all other possible solutions, we were forced to drive our hot car to the nearest motel and check in for the night. I called my father-in-law in Bryan about our predicament and he came to our rescue. He would have one of his cars mounted on a flatbed tow truck immediately and driven to our motel.

It was now 11:30 P.M., and we were almost three hours from home. We got to bed around midnight. At two, there was a knock on our door. I got up and helped unload Patty's father's car and then hoist ours up for the return trip on the tow truck. It's early morning now; dawn's breaking, my family's asleep, and I'm wide awake.

We're lucky, I guess, that I was able to travel with them. Patty wouldn't have noticed the gauge rising and more than likely she and the boys would have gotten stranded along the highway. The travel in this game sure is exciting.

Monday, June 25
Toledo

Maybe I'm better off relieving. I got my spot start tonight and I was gassed after all of forty pitches. I knew beforehand Joe wasn't going to let me go long, but I was surprised how quickly I got tired. I gave up four runs in the third inning and was only able to go one more inning. I'm not offering the number of pitches as an excuse. I wouldn't have had to throw so many if I hadn't tossed volleyball-sized fastballs in the third.

If there's any place to have a poor outing, though, it's Toledo. I was showered by game's end and ready to go home. It was nice to hop in the car—a healthy car—and get away from baseball for a while. There's no better place to reinforce priorities than home. There was no baseball talk on the ride there. Win or lose, we very seldom dwell on baseball in our family. It's always been that way between Patty and me.

I have to admit I'm fighting with my attitude right now. It's not due to tonight's game either. It's been going on for days. I realize by admitting this I run the risk of adding fuel to the skeptics' fire: "No wonder he was never able to accomplish more in his career. He's not persistent enough. That'd never happen to old Charlie Hustle."

It's not a flaw that jumps out at people. It's a struggle within, and I know what the problem is. I've had the opportunity to spend a lot of time with Patty and the boys lately, and I like it. I like it enough that I don't want to leave it. I can still make my body do all the running and exercises, but sometimes my brain is elsewhere. It happens to others, too, from time to time. Don't people in most occupations suffer occasional dry spells?

Believe it or not, I don't *want* to be like Pete Rose, even putting aside the gambling thing. If that's viewed as a weakness, so be it. I don't believe that admitting and dealing with human emotions diminishes a person's competitiveness anyway. I gave it everything I had tonight. I got beat because I threw bad pitches, not because I love my family.

Tuesday, June 26
Toledo

My attitude is no better today. I didn't want to go to the park. More accurately, I didn't want to leave home.

I was talking about all this today with Dwight Lowry—fellow father, fellow turd—and he understood perfectly. My attitude will probably bounce back once I get away from home.

I cling to any semblance of a normal home life, but I have to work through my indifference and push myself during the final two months. My problem is *not* how much I hate going to the park at all; it's how much I hate leaving everything behind. But I'll be all right. I don't wear my heart on my sleeve, and I don't take it to the mound.

Wednesday, June 27
Toledo

We were swept by Toledo, losing 4–0 tonight. We're now 0–6 with seven more games before we return to Indy. This has the makings of a disastrous trip.

There was some news today, and I'd like to see it as good news. Howard Farmer was called up, and I may get his slot in the rotation. "As far as I know," Joe Kerrigan said, "and until I hear otherwise, you'll take Howard's turn. They may want to bring up somebody else from Double-A to start. I won't know anything for sure until I talk to Rick Williams."

Howard's thrown better lately—obviously well enough in Montreal's minds to get the call. Often, a club goes with who's hot at the time, which only makes sense. The last two weeks, Howard's been as productive as any starter in our unproductive rotation. He's pitching with confidence and seems closer to fulfilling his potential.

I have a hypothetical question. If Howard had struggled a bit lately, but he still had Scott's numbers, would he still go up? Probably. *Now*, if Scott were showing some signs of coming around, and *he* was saddled with Howard's stats, would he go? I don't know. I'd like to be able to say, "Of course not. This game's so unfair and I know because I've been repeatedly victimized by it." I can't go that far, not with a clear conscience. The game's more fair than I sometimes think. Don't most people, though, have times when they think they haven't gotten a totally fair shake at work? Don't most people have *careers* like that?

Transactions, at least in my business, are too unpredictable for any employee to always see the pattern. Justice is often served, but I've witnessed too many moves to accept on faith the wisdom of every decision.

Right or wrong, this was an *easy* move to make. Howard has been pitching better, but "Howard Farmer" is the name Indy wants to recommend, and more importantly, "Howard Farmer" is the name Montreal wants to hear. From an organizational standpoint, the best move is one in which everybody gets a pat on the back.

Thursday, June 28
Des Moines

We had the type of travel day that is often associated with minor league baseball. We were supposed to leave Toledo at 8:57 this morning and arrive in Chicago at 9:09, allowing us plenty of time to catch our ten o'clock flight to Des Moines.

It didn't work that way. Our plane was delayed nearly two hours out of Toledo, so we missed our connecting flight in Chicago. There were two later flights offered by the same airline to Des Moines, but both were booked solid. We sat at our would-be gate for an hour and a half while our trainer, John Spinosa, negotiated with the ticket agents. Some guys played cards, some had their headphones on, some read, and others just sat around and picked their noses. Finally, John emerged with tickets—tickets worth seven dollars at any eatery in O'Hare. This meant I could get a few cookies, a hot dog, and a small drink, or use it as a down payment on a real meal.

John also told us we had a flight to Des Moines, but it was on another airline and departed from a gate only minutes away—by cab. We still had three hours before it left, so we had ample time to walk.

After lounging at our new gate, we boarded our plane—but only after all the scheduled passengers were seated. We got stuck in whatever seats were left. We landed in Des Moines at 4:30 P.M., six hours later than planned. Just like the big leaguers, we didn't have to mess with our luggage. It had arrived on an earlier flight with our original airline.

We bused to our hotel, regrouped, and headed for the park, where we lost our seventh straight game. We took vans back to the hotel after the game. Most of us are a little weary.

Today was *so* exciting.

Friday, June 29
Des Moines

It's been finalized: I'll fill Howard's vacancy in the starting rotation, at least for now. Upon hearing the news, I got back into
my old routine. I normally run a lot, but as a reliever I couldn't
pound out five miles a couple hours before game time and
expect to be strong if I were needed in the second inning.

I went to the park early, put my running shoes on, secured
my headphones to my ears with the traditional sanitary sock
tied around my head, and hit the open road. I was a vegetable
after three miles. Still, I look forward to working my legs back
into the shape I'm comfortable with. I missed the regimenta-
tion that starting allowed me. I felt guilty as a reliever; I never
felt I was doing enough.

I have a new pitch to go along with my old role. I learned a
split-finger the last two days and will break it out Sunday in
Omaha. I have nothing to lose by throwing it. What's the worst
that can happen? I don't make it back to the big leagues? I get
taken out of the rotation? The only pressure I have here is
what I put upon myself. There are no great expectations from
the Expos placed on me. That's not to say I feel no pressure or
don't expect to make it to Montreal. It's the mission to get to
Montreal that supplies the pressure.

It's a self-induced mission, though. The Expos have mis-
sions of their own. But I know the split-finger has salvaged
many careers, and if I thought it was impossible to return to
the big leagues, I wouldn't be as excited about the new pitch
as I am. But the one certainty is that I'll never know unless I
try, and that's why I keep going. If I do walk away from baseball,
I'm going to do it knowing I've done everything I can control.

Saturday, June 30
Des Moines

We had another charming travel day. It was worth the price, though. We had just endured fourteen innings tonight before beating Iowa 4–3, our first win on this trip after losing the previous eight. And I could have been even more excited about it had I entered the game. Not as a pitcher, either. When our bench became thin late in the game I was again told to go put my spikes on. Sadly, I again didn't get the call to pinch-hit. But I always get juiced about the chance.

It was still a good win for us and our guys celebrated afterward like we'd won a playoff game.

That was at 12:30 A.M.

We left Des Moines by bus at 1:15 A.M. and arrived here in Omaha at 3:45. I counted on getting some sleep along the way, but the spaghetti we were served after the game—warm after nine innings, icy after fourteen—spun around in my stomach like a pasta rock.

When we got here I turned the thermostat to ninety and went straight to bed with all the covers over me. Scott thought I was crazy, but I had the chills: food poisoning, I thought. After a rough night, I got up around eight-thirty, bleary but on the mend.

Sammy called and after talking to Scott for a few minutes he remembered his original intention was to wish me good luck. Scott and I went to breakfast and now I'm waiting to go to the park for our afternoon game. There'll be some tired men out on the field today, although it probably won't catch up with us until after the game.

One more note worth mentioning. John Costello has been back with us from the Expos for a week now. There are so many moves made here that if I reported them all the book would have to be printed in agate type. I don't think John's here on rehab again; I think he just couldn't get anyone out. I could be wrong, though. There are too many changes to track down all the stories that lie behind them.

July

Sunday, July 1
Omaha

Our winning streak continued this afternoon. We beat Omaha 3–1 in a heated contest; it was over 100 degrees. I had one of my better games of the year. I went 7⅔ innings, allowed five hits, the one run, walked one, and struck out eight. I felt strong and could have finished the game, but Tim and Joe obviously thought I'd had enough. I've struck out seventeen in my last fifteen innings. That's over a third of my total for the year. Since I cut back on the throwing I do between outings, my arm has found new life. I again reached 90 mph occasionally, 88–89 consistently. I had a tight slider, too, which always helps. I used seven split-fingers and recorded three outs with them.

After games like this, I think I'd be stupid to quit at the end of the season. As with all jobs, baseball has its ups and downs. With baseball, the gratification is instantaneous. But so is the discouragement. Even through the bad times, there's the knowledge that, however modest my ability, baseball is what I do best.

Patty is well aware of this, too. When we talk about life after baseball, we love the idea of being together as a family. But we get a little scared when we discuss just how I'll support that togetherness. The simple truth is that we have absolutely no clue as to what I'll be able to find for a job. My resume has its weaknesses; not a lot of corporations advertise for pitchers.

An outing like today's reinforces my belief that I can and should pitch in the major leagues again. That's what it ought to do. That's what I'm here for. People tell me I shouldn't quit after this season, that I may even get back to the big leagues this year. At times like this, I feel it'd be illogical for me to retire as long as I have ability to offer.

Then I stop that train of thought and wonder if I feel that way only because it allows me to put off dealing with my uncertain future outside of the game.

Monday, July 2
Omaha

I was awakened early this morning by the phone. It was the manager of the Milan baseball club in Italy. I was more than half asleep for the first part of the conversation and I thought someone was playing a cruel joke on me.

Even had I been wide awake, I'd have had the same suspicions. The guy wanted to know if I had any interest in pitching for him next year over in Italy. Each Italian team is allowed two American players. One is always a pitcher. They play three games a week, Friday through Sunday, and have two workouts during the other days, which amounts to little more than batting practice. An American pitcher is permitted to throw only once a week. That means I'd start a game over the weekend and throw on the side once during the week, with two days completely free of any baseball. They'd give me the use of a car and a furnished apartment. They would, of course, pay for my transportation to and from Italy. The manager didn't want or expect any commitment right now. He just wanted to find out if there was any interest on my part. I told him I'd like to know more about the operation and that he was more than welcome to call me at home following this season. He said he looked forward to talking to me again, and we hung up.

He'd been pretty vague where money was concerned. That would naturally have to be ironed out to our satisfaction. I'd ask, too, for transportation there and back for my family. At first I thought the idea was ridiculous, but as the day went on, I found myself warming up to the idea. It might give me a great final chapter to my career. It would certainly be a once-in-a-lifetime opportunity. It could be educational for all of us. Who knows? I haven't talked to Patty yet. My gut feeling is that she won't be crazy about the idea. I've told a couple of friends about it, and they think I should look into it.

We'll see what happens.

Tuesday, July 3
Omaha

Howard Farmer made his major league debut last night as the Expos hosted Atlanta. He went 4⅓ innings, gave up eight hits, six runs, walked two, and struck out two. The Braves hit four home runs off him. What that proves is absolutely nothing.

For me to write how I—or anyone else here—could have done better is stupid. The Expos certainly aren't going to look at Howard's performance and say, "Gee, this kid doesn't belong here." That wouldn't be right. And it'd be just as wrong for any of us in Indianapolis to assume we'd have enjoyed a better fate.

Howard can hardly be judged on 4⅓ innings, especially when it's his first major league outing. It's my guess that Montreal will watch Howard closely for a couple more games and if things don't get better, they'll make another move. The Expos are in a pennant race, and they simply cannot afford a weak link in their chain, even if it happens to be their top prospect. There are ways to hide a starter in the big leagues when scheduling allows it. At times, there are enough days off to permit a team to go with a four-man rotation and keep the wobbly fifth wheel sidelined.

The news of Howard's poor outing was received in contrasting fashion here. The younger, brighter-eyed pitchers tried to guess how Montreal will react to Howard's "failure," and they speculated about what that could mean for each of them. The more experienced pitchers took it more in stride.

This is the last day of our longest road trip of the year. We won three and lost ten and have once again cemented ourselves in last place. August is a tough month to endure when a team has nothing at stake. There is not one off day scheduled during the last six weeks of our season.

Wednesday, July 4
Indianapolis

With the media attention that's focused on athletes, it's easy for a fan to be awed by prominent sports figures. The hero worship is really not that difficult to comprehend. It's the way professional sports are designed. People who really make a difference in the world—doctors, scientists, teachers, civil-rights leaders, whatever—get assessed as people. Ballplayers too often get assessed as heroes.

I think it'd be interesting to conduct a survey across America and ask two questions, "Who plays right field for the Oakland A's?" and "Who's the U.S. Secretary of State?" I can't pretend to forecast who'd be more recognizable, but it'd be fun finding out. I suppose it's not a fair comparison, anyway. After all, James Baker has never even made the 30-30 club, let alone the 40-40.

The first time I met a "superstar" was in spring training of '79. I was in big league camp with San Diego and spent the first couple weeks marveling at my surroundings. Randy Jones was the ace of the staff back then, and I remember thinking that I threw a *lot* harder than he did. I'd watch him throw on

132

the side and just shake my head in disbelief. Of course, at that time, I thought corners were something you found at the end of a street; I was so unimpressed by his velocity that I didn't notice the bottom falling out of every pitch he threw. I thought there was nothing to be gained from watching a pitcher like him.

Then one day a tap came on my shoulder. "You wanna work with me a little bit?" said a deep voice. I turned around and saw an Adam's apple, glanced upward, and found its owner to be Dave Winfield.

"Sure," I said. Great! I thought. Winnie (as we Padres called him) is going to work with me! This is what I need. Hands-on instructions with an all-star. This man was drafted in three sports by four different teams, and was the best everyday player with the Padres. What an opportunity!

We made our way to the batting cages and he asked me where I was from. "Ohio," I said. Having played college basketball at Minnesota, Dave automatically defended his participation in an ugly fight that took place years before on the court between Minnesota and Ohio State. I don't care if you *started* the fight, I thought, just share your baseball knowledge with me. You play teacher and I'll play student.

Dave handed me a bucket of balls and walked toward the home-plate end of the cage, bat in hand. I knew then what my role was in this working relationship. I was the feeder. I dumped balls into the pitching machine so he could hit. I sat behind a net and ducked under line drives as they ricocheted off the surrounding sides. He hit a couple buckets, we picked the balls up, and we were finished.

Friday, July 6
Indianapolis

Tim and Joe have been simmering for most of the year watching us play. Tonight they finally boiled over. Louisville swept us at home, including tonight's 8–2 loss. I started and went seven innings, giving up five hits, four runs and three walks, striking out three. I threw a hanging slider for a two-run homer in the fifth. If the umpire had one more eye, he'd have been a cyclops. Admittedly, though, he wasn't any better for Louisville's pitchers.

Louisville scored four runs off our bullpen in the eighth inning. I was in the clubhouse icing my shoulder at the time, but I heard that our guys weren't pitching very aggressively. Combine that with our lack of run production lately, and you come up with an enraged manager and a ballistic pitching coach.

Tim went first. "You guys are horseshit!" he yelled. "You're an embarrassment. I'm not going to put up with this anymore!" His speech serves only as an introduction to what he does best. Tim is more demonstrative by nature. After a couple more verbal assaults, he picked up a good-sized laundry cart and heaved it against a wall, jarring several Indian artifacts to the floor. He was finished.

Then it was Joe's turn. His volume was turned up, maybe all the way to eleven. "I have a few things I'd like to say to the team concerning our pitching staff." He then walked over and faced all us pitchers. "I'm sick and tired of seeing our catchers set up inside and then watching you guys miss by three feet outside! I'm sick of the oh-two base hits! I'm tired of the complaining!" he complained. "You guys want to know where the problem lies? It's inside of you. Most of you don't have any guts! You're empty! I hear some of you guys bitching about how you should be in the big leagues. You can't even pitch here! I promise you this: if I hear any more of your shit, I'll bury you. I've got the power to do it, and so does Tim. Be dressed tomorrow at three-thirty." By the end, he was screaming.

The clubhouse stayed quiet just a little while, and then the players headed for the showers.

Joe approached me after everybody had left the clubhouse and said he thought I had good stuff tonight and the slider hurt me. He felt the split-finger worked real well, too. I think his day was a lot worse than mine.

Saturday, July 7
Louisville

We bused to Louisville this morning and got in a little after noon. The pitchers had enough time to grab a bite to eat, relax for an hour or so, and then catch a 2:30 van to the park. Usually, when we're asked to be at the park early, we wonder what Joe's going to do with us. Today, as we waited in the hotel lobby, it was more, "What's Joe going to do *to* us?"

When we got to the park, Joe told us to put on our running attire. That in itself eliminated the possibility of bodily harm by means of the fungo. Then we had a short meeting in right field. "We're not possibly as bad as we've been pitching lately," Joe said. "Tim and I are told constantly how we have nothing to work with here. I won't accept that. I *can't* accept that, because I see the potential that we have here. I know our capabilities, and we're simply falling way short of it. I hang with you guys on every single pitch, and—I'll tell you, fellas—some of the pitches you've been throwing up toward the plate have been awfully hard to take. I'm at a loss, but I had two outstanding pitching coaches when I played, and when things got like this, they dealt with it the old-fashioned way: they ran our asses into the ground. And that's exactly what *we're* going to do. We can all use it. It'll be good therapy for you and it'll also be good therapy for me."

We ran over twenty liners. Redbird Stadium is carpeted, so the heat was intensified. Joe ran every step with us. He really does live and die with every pitcher out on the mound. In the previous years at Indianapolis, he must have been on a constant high because his staffs were always nothing short of dominating. This year, his policy remains the same, but his staff seldom provides any sense of accomplishment for him.

It's got to be tempting for him to do as some pitching coaches would and alienate himself from us. He never has, though. He shares our disappointment—and our running.

As would be expected, some guys handled the running better than others. I run more on my own than what Joe put us through today, so it didn't bother me. I don't usually agree with the old-school approach, but I thought our therapy session today was exactly what was needed.

Sunday, July 8
Louisville

Patty and I were married nine years ago today in Hawaii, back when I was in Triple-A for the Padres. As with so many other anniversaries, we'll spend this one apart. I suppose we could have waited until after the season to get married. That would have allowed us to celebrate our anniversaries together. July 8 is only a date, though. We'll be just as separated on July 9.

I had a plant delivered to the house and sent her a card. She has more pressing matters on her mind right now than our anniversary. She could deliver the baby at any time. With the muggy weather lately, she's been miserable much of the time. The boys are now adjusted to their summer activities and are always ready to exhaust what little energy she has left. She's holding up well, but she really has no choice.

Sometimes I feel so guilty because I'm removed from a period in her life that really ought to be shared. I don't think I'm really feeling regrets about our past. It's more like wishful thinking about our present.

The pitchers had another meeting this afternoon in the manager's office. Joe usually addresses the pitchers, but today he handed it over to Tim.

"Changes are going to take place," he said. "There aren't going to be any moves with our pitching staff, so you guys are all safe—for the time being. All I can tell you is what I see. Louisville has .210 hitters swinging out of their ass against us, like they know what's coming. I'm not telling you to hit anybody, but we have to establish the inside part of the plate, and if that means knocking somebody down, that's what we'll have to do. They're too comfortable in the batter's box."

Joe concluded the meeting by citing a couple pitchers as examples of how we're pitching and suggested we impart a little more fear into the hitters' minds.

Monday, July 9
Louisville

The Indianapolis Indians hit a new low tonight. We fought admirably throughout the game and scored in the top of the ninth to take a one-run lead. With stopper Bob Malloy on the mound for us, we had good reason to be optimistic—we thought. Louisville scored twice before we even got an out. They've beaten us six games in a row. Tim got thrown out of his first game this year by the home-plate umpire, which, indirectly, redeems me, because it was the same blind man I had behind the plate three nights ago. His strike zone is shaped like an upright egg.

I may have messed up my season today. While taking my workout, I strained my pectoralis major, which is a muscle that runs under the armpit. It's the same place I injured in '86 and it took forever to heal back then. By the time it did heal fully, in early '87, the next thing I knew I was out of baseball.

I guess the best way to describe how I feel now is scared. There's pain I can throw with and there's pain I can do nothing with. If I damaged the muscle severely, I'm out for a long time, and there isn't a whole lot of season left—and there may not be a whole lot of career left.

It's not good news, but worrying won't help. We have the next two days off for the All-Star break, and I'll spend them back home in Ohio. I'll occupy enough time pampering and worrying about Patty to keep from being consumed with my arm. How noble of me. I have anti-inflammatories to take and weight routines to follow, so I'll do what I can, and we'll add it to our prayers. I'm supposed to toss a few balls on Wednesday to see how it feels. My next scheduled start is Friday. I'd rather dwell on going home for a couple days. We have weeds in our yard that are laughing at me, as well as a hefty list of other chores Patty will have compiled. I can't wait.

Tuesday, July 10
Bryan, Ohio

I think about my shoulder more often than I'd like, but not nearly as much as I would if I were at the park nine or ten hours a day.

We had a fun day together and tonight we celebrated the days off with dinner at Kaufman's, my father-in-law's restaurant. There have been occasions over the years when my appetite has been the direct beneficiary of the family I married into. That's to be expected, and I offer no apologies for it. People often profit from positions held or abilities possessed by their parents or in-laws.

Greg Booker certainly did. In 1982 Greg was pitching at the A-ball level for the Padres in Reno. These are his numbers for that year:

W—L	ERA	IP	H	BB	SO
8–13	6.35	162	160	157	81

I've seen many players get released after a year like that, especially at the A-ball level. Greg was not only retained the following year, he was promoted—to Triple-A. Do you feel his numbers were deserving of such a move? And while you're thinking, consider that the Padres tended to move players up slowly and methodically. Tony Gwynn advanced through the various levels rapidly, but he may very well be a Hall of Famer someday. Nobody ever doubted that Tony should be advanced. Kevin McReynolds went up fairly fast, but he, too, has since shown why. During my years with the Padres, those three guys were pushed up the ladder faster than anyone. Greg Booker, though, is hardly in the same league as Tony Gwynn and Kevin McReynolds. He is, however, the son-in-law of Jack McKeon, then San Diego's general manager.

In '83, I was second in the league with fourteen wins for Las Vegas, San Diego's new Triple-A affiliate. Greg was also on that team. These are his stats:

W—L	ERA	IP	H	BB	SO
5–6	5.45	102	120	68	58

We were both called up in September. The Padres rewarded me with five innings, in which I gave up only one run. In contrast, Greg was a workhorse. He got 11⅔ innings—and gave up eighteen hits, nine earned runs, and nine walks.

Since that time, Greg has spent the better part of the next six seasons in San Diego. He was traded to the Twins in '89 and pitched in the big leagues for them—for days. I don't know what the problem was in Minnesota. Maybe he had arm problems. Maybe he couldn't find the strike zone. Or maybe he'd just run out of connections.

Nobody held this against Greg. He was one of the more popular players on the team. What's he going to say? "No thanks, Dad. I'd rather stay in A ball. Calling me up won't look good. Other guys might get ticked off." It was a great break for Greg. It also has to be the most blatant display of nepotism I've ever seen firsthand.

Wednesday, July 11
Bryan, Ohio

I'm hours removed from the ballpark and I spent the entire day wearing out Joey and Sammy. I tested my arm by throwing bombs to the boys with a Nerf football. It was feeling better. I did absolutely nothing constructive around the house, which delighted the boys—and me. I kept the boys out of Patty's hair; we all went down to the basement and, as always, they asked me to put on a wild song. They chose the B-52's "Cosmic Thing," a favorite of theirs, and I cranked it up. We all did the worm. You had to be there to appreciate it.

Thursday, July 12
Indianapolis

I headed for Indianapolis around noon today so I could be at the park early enough to have my arm examined and be dressed in time for a three-o'clock pitchers' workout. I've left my family behind hundreds of times over the years, but I've never become comfortable with it. The boys were both crying as they stood beside Patty, waving good-bye. Her due date is tomorrow.

We play in Indy for the next week, and I promised Patty that I'd be back home within four hours of her first contraction. In previous years, the distance between us has always been much farther: closer to four days than four hours.

The arm seems to be improving. My range of motion is better and I threw about half-speed today with no pain. Joe juggled the rotation to give me a couple extra days. "As of right now," he said, "you're penciled in to start Sunday. I say 'penciled' because that's subject to change. The Expos may make a move with Howard, since Tim Burke came off the disabled list in Montreal. If Howard does come down, he'll start Sunday instead."

So I was back in limbo. Then Howard showed up during our game. Now I'm in serious limbo. When will I pitch next? Will I be able to pitch? Will I start? Will I return to the pen? Who knows? Again, perspective comes into play.

When I was sent to the bullpen a few weeks ago I was upset. Now with my arm a bit tender, I'm not nearly as concerned about *how* I'll be used; I wonder if I *can* be used. Athletes often take health for granted. Not me, at least not now.

Saturday, July 14
Indianapolis

It's now the time of year when players must decide—or at least consider—whether they want to play winter ball. Every organization I've been with passes around a winter ball sign-up sheet. But just because a player wants to play winter ball doesn't necessarily mean he'll be invited. Teams in Puerto Rico, Venezuela, and the Dominican Republic are permitted only a small number of American players. More guys want to play than get to play. Montreal ran its sign-up sheet through the clubhouse today. Rick Williams and Joe Kerrigan are both approaching pitchers they'd like to see play and answering questions from interested players. I'm not in either category anymore.

I've pitched winter ball twice, both times in Puerto Rico. The first time was '81 for the Mayaguez Indios. Patty and I were married earlier that year in Hawaii and looked at Puerto Rico as a wonderful opportunity for an extended honeymoon. I had enjoyed a very successful first season at the Triple-A level in Honolulu and had been called up to San Diego in September, where I pitched well in each of my four starts. Padres officials told me that winter ball would enhance my chances for the following season. It seemed both the logical and fun thing to do.

After the major league season was completed, I flew home from San Diego. Patty and I had a belated wedding reception the following evening. Two days later, after storing all of our wedding gifts, we were on a jet to San Juan.

We got to San Juan and then caught a small propeller plane, sometimes referred to in the baseball world as a "knuckleball express," which took us through a terrible thunderstorm and, somehow, delivered us to the other side of the island.

We thought we were through with our ordeal. Hardly. We were met at the airport and driven to our condo. The Indios told us that ours was the nicest and cleanest of all those offered to the American players. The owner of our condo was a doctor.

He certainly wasn't a hygienist. We opened the door to our place and discovered a filthy dungeon, caked-on grime coating every inch of the walls and carpets and countertops. I can't even begin to describe the bathroom.

Patty and I didn't say ten words to each other for the next three hours. We broke out some mops and buckets and trash bags, and we cleaned until we met each other in the middle of the room, and then we went to bed—on our own sheets, of course. Everything that was supposed to be provided wasn't, except a car, which we shared with my best man, Eric Show, and his wife, Cara Mia.

We complained to the team until they reimbursed us for the essentials—towels, sheets, dishes, silverware, pillows; you name it, we had to buy it. A week of continued cleaning and a few hundred bucks later, we were settled for the next three months.

We became friends with all my teammates and their wives, including Walt Terrell, Brett Butler, Von Hayes, Matt Sinatro, and the Shows. As promised, it was a terrific experience, although I don't believe the baseball end of it matched what Patty and I learned off the field. For instance, we had no previous experience chasing salamanders from our home every morning or dodging the frogs that covered the sidewalks each night. We'd see dozens of kids walking around with handkerchiefs over their noses. We soon learned the cloth was saturated with paint thinner and they were getting high off it. We found how difficult it is to communicate in another language. What we learned more than anything was to appreciate what we have here in the States.

I returned to Puerto Rico, alone, in '85. I joined the season in progress and pitched for the San Juan Metros. The accommodations were much better and the travel wasn't nearly as time-consuming with San Juan as my base. I started a couple games and felt something in my forearm. The team sent me to a doctor. I wasn't warm in my seat before he asked, "Well, do you want a shot?"—meaning cortisone. I got out of there as soon as I could. If I was going to blow my arm out or get a shot for it, it was going to happen back home, not there.

Some guys love winter ball. Others, like me, aren't drawn to it. I think its importance is overrated. Younger players are told that going down there and putting up great numbers could help them the following spring. Of course, it *could*. So could resting their bodies for the winter. Suppose there are two hitters of equal ability, Mike and Bill. Mike goes to Puerto Rico and hits the cover off the ball. Bill stays home for the winter. The following spring they're both fighting for one open spot on a roster. Mike loses his stroke, as hitters will, while Bill shows up at camp and crushes everything tossed toward the plate. Is that organization going to take Mike north with them because he hit well in San Juan? I doubt it.

Sunday, July 15
Indianapolis

Some reporter asked me today what has been the highlight of my career. It's a common question when writers are fishing around for feature stories. Although I don't have hundreds of memories to choose from, there are a few incidents I'll always remember, and this is the story I told the guy.

In the fall of '83 I was called up to San Diego. I got all of five innings' work into the entire month of September, but there is one confrontation that only I can claim.

I was called upon to finish out a game against the Cincinnati Reds in San Diego. I threw the eighth with no problem. When I came out for the ninth, there was a little more electricity in the air. I had no idea what was going on and went ahead with my warm-up tosses. Soon the large crowd assembled at Jack Murphy Stadium began to chant, but I had more important matters to tend to and couldn't decipher what they were saying. I disposed of the first two hitters and then the chant turned to a roar. I felt good out there, but I doubted that the fans' fascination was channeled toward number 62 on the mound.

I finally figured out what was going on. It all came together for me when the next batter stepped out of the dugout. Johnny Bench was making his last appearance in San Diego before retiring. He'd had a string of impressive final at-bats in other cities and the Padres fans wanted one last look at the future Hall of Famer, something that'd make a good story for the grandkids someday. Bench wasn't in the lineup that day, but the Reds graciously gave the people what they wanted. He came out to the on-deck circle to pinch-hit. The place erupted. Bench stepped into the batter's box and I got the sign from Terry Kennedy.

Bench took the first fastball for strike one. He was late on the next fastball for strike two. I knew what the crowd wanted. They wanted to see Johnny Bench jack a seven-hundred-foot homer—off me. Terry again called for a fastball with the 0–2 count. I wound up and threw it as hard as I could, which, back then, was pretty hard. Bench was late again. I struck him out on three consecutive fastballs.

The fans booed me. I walked back to our dugout, wondering whether the Israelites had cheered Goliath and booed David. But I knew, deep down, that they weren't booing me at all. They were booing their disallowed wishes.

Terry Kennedy shared their disappointment. He came up to me and said, "I was sitting right down the middle on all three fastballs. I wanted him to hit one out."

"Thanks, Terry." I had to laugh.

Monday, July 16
Indianapolis

Rick Williams was in town again today. While the rest of the pitchers were bunting, he and I walked through the outfield and shagged stray balls. He carried his fungo bat with him and hit the balls back to the mound. "Watch this," he said. "Right on the green." Sure enough, the ball came to a stop not six feet from the rubber.

Rick wanted to know if there was anything on my mind.

"Now that you mention it there is," I said. "Am I wasting my time or kidding myself by thinking there's a chance I could get up to Montreal?"

When he paused to search for the right words, I knew what he had to say wouldn't be encouraging. "I wouldn't count on it happening, Fire. I don't mean to discourage you, and I could be wrong. You've pitched well and your numbers are good, but I'd estimate your chances to be very slim. Like I said, I could be wrong. I know that's not what you wanted to hear. I'm just being honest."

"If you'd have said anything else," I said, "I'd have been suspicious." I told him I appreciated his honesty.

And then he hit a few more perfect shots to the edge of the mound, and we changed the subject to something more important—we swapped childbirth stories. His wife has had the type of short and uncomplicated labors Patty dreams about.

Patty's now three days overdue. She wasn't feeling real well this afternoon, so I asked Tim if I could have an extra day at home added on to our scheduled day off tomorrow. Not only was I granted Wednesday, but I was also given permission to leave Indy today, as soon as I tested my arm on the side with Joe.

The workout went okay. I could still feel some pain, but the arm was much improved. I'm slated to start the second game of a doubleheader on Thursday, so hopefully it'll be fully recovered by then. As I iced my arm after throwing, both Tim and Joe went out of their way to assure me, again, that I had their blessings to do whatever was needed at home. "Don't worry about the game on Thursday," Tim said. "Just give us a call if you can't make it. The family comes first."

I'd told Rick earlier in the afternoon that Montreal was the best organization I'd been with. As a player I base my evaluation on knowledge, instruction, and communication of management and coaches I come in contact with.

"We have our problems here," Rick said. "Just like any other organization. I don't think we have as many, though."

I think he's right. I may question their responses to certain circumstances, but baseball is a business, a big business. As with any business, employees are sometimes going to complain about who does and does not climb the corporate ladder. Montreal's not a perfect enterprise; what is? Besides, if I can only degrade and never find positive attributes, I'm flirting with considering myself perfect. I'm hardly perfect. Sometimes it's tough for me to admit, but my story is a very small chapter in a very large book.

Wednesday, July 18
Bryan, Ohio

Shortly after six this morning, Thomas John Fireovid was born. Mother and child are doing fine. Patty had a much better delivery this time around. Her previous two labors were both over twenty hours. Each time, the Lamaze-class techniques went out the window before she was halfway done.

She was in labor for just five hours with Tommy, although I suppose no woman would use the word "just" in any sentence discussing the duration of her labor. Still, Patty had an easy time, at least in comparison. Tommy checked in, with a full head of hair, at seven pounds, seven ounces and nineteen inches. He's a pretty neat little guy.

They're both resting now. I thought I'd called everyone in the family, but later in the day realized I'd forgotten my sister and one of Patty's brothers. I stopped at Kaufman's for lunch. Patty's mom must have already announced Tommy's birth to every person in the place. "Tommy John, huh?" more than one of the people commented. "Did you name him after the pitcher?" I don't think so. Maybe at some extremely deep subconscious level I wish I were lefthanded. Actually, we've liked Thomas as a first name for a long time, and John's my father's name. We tend to favor the less cosmic or trendy names for our own. Joseph. Samuel. Thomas. What some look at as generic we see as solid. A rose by any other name . . .

146

I called Tim in Indy and assured him I'd pitch in tomorrow night's doubleheader. He's been so understanding, I feel that the least I can do is drive there and start a game for him. It'll really bum me out if I drive to Indy and my arm can't answer the bell.

I told Sammy today that it still hasn't hit me that I'm a father again. He frowned. "Why would Tommy want to hit you, Daddy?" Blessed are the literal-minded.

It probably won't hit me, actually, until the season is over and I'm at home on a daily basis. Of course, I'm happy and thankful beyond words. But I'll also spend only a few days in Tommy's presence over the next month and a half. That bothers me and I *know* it upsets Patty.

I'm tired now. But I'm a veteran dad; I know enough to keep my mouth shut. The last thing Patty would want to hear now is how exhausted *I* am.

Thursday, July 19
Bryan and Indianapolis

The boys were fired up this morning. The hospital allows a half-hour visitation by siblings upon arrangement and today was their day to meet their new little brother. I cleaned them up, packed the video camera, and together we went to see Mom and Tommy.

I was eager to see their initial reaction, but there wasn't any. They just stared. Eventually, they loosened up and even took turns holding him. Joey said Tommy was "awesome" and Sammy thought he was "cool." Patty and I tried to explain that the baby will bring a whole new definition to the word "gentle." By the visit's end, the boys seemed comfortable with Tommy. Probably too comfortable. We couldn't stay long and soon had to leave. The boys begged to take their gowns with them so they could pretend to be doctors at home, but I denied their request.

I took them home and a little later Grandma Kaufman picked

up Joey, who'd decided to stay with his grandparents. I wasn't at all disappointed that the boys were separated today. It's much easier to keep an eye on just one of them. Sammy and I ran some stuff back up to the hospital for Patty and then had a late lunch before the two of us drove to Indianapolis.

Sammy rode all the way there with his Indians uniform packed in his duffel bag.

I left in plenty of time to get there by the beginning of the first game, but—with a rest-room stop here, a beverage fill-up there, yet another bathroom stop here—we were a little late. During the season, I sometimes forget that people traveling with kids are always a little late.

We got to the clubhouse halfway through the first game. I put some heat on my arm and then went to get dressed. Sammy was too shy to change into his uniform in front of others, so I finished putting my uniform on with him in a bathroom stall. The first game was completed about a half-hour later and I quickly turned Sammy over to Scott Anderson, who was going to sit with him in the stands. "We'll be fine," he said. "My wife brought some doughnuts for him." Great, I thought. Massive doses of sugar are sure to bring out the best in the boy.

I hurried out to the bullpen, where Joe Kerrigan was waiting. I ran three sprints, touched my toes, and warmed up. My shoulder was stiff early in the game. I gave up a run in the first and in the second, but the stiffness worked itself out and I retired Denver in order until one out in the final inning. I finished the game and threw well, walking one and striking out three. We lost 2–1. Scott said my fastball was at 83–84 in the first two innings, but I topped out at 90 in the last. Afterward, I had to ice my shoulder and talk to reporters. I asked Joe if he knew what my role was. He laughed. "I don't know," he said. "There might be a move coming up that'll allow you to stay in the rotation. We've got a split [day-night] doubleheader on Sunday in Nashville. I might need you. Give me a call on Saturday, and I'll let you know if we want you there."

I sure hope they don't. It was midnight before Sammy and I left the park. We ordered some burgers at a drive-through and went to the apartment.

We have a family rule against the boys coming into bed with Mommy and Daddy, and usually when they're in Indy, they sleep in a tent on the floor. Once, each of us had our pajamas on, and Sammy got a meek look in his big brown eyes. "Is it okay if I sleep in your bed?" he asked—in a way that made it sound like he thought I'd say no, a way that left me no other answer but yes. I didn't *want* to give him any other answer but yes.

"Yes," I said.

He smiled and crawled into bed and we turned out the lights and fell asleep together.

Friday, July 20
Bryan, Ohio

It's been a big day for the Fireovids. I got up pretty early and went through my usual morning routine. I let Sammy sleep in, but I'll admit I wasn't tiptoeing around the apartment. I was anxious to get back to Bryan because Patty and the baby are supposed to come home today and I'm supposed to pick them up at the hospital. Sammy eventually woke up, and we went out for breakfast before driving home. I was determined to make good time. I already had a drink ready for him, and I grabbed a large, empty glass container from the apartment to act as a travel potty for him if needed. Fortunately, it wasn't. We pulled into Bryan around noon and I dropped Sammy off with his grandparents.

I rushed into the hospital and checked in on Patty. She'd received a lot of flower arrangements, so I carted them out to the car, and a nurse wheeled her out with Tommy. I got every-body and everything situated. We drove out to her parents' house, picked up the boys, and went home. Patty and the baby retired to the bedroom. The three of us guys fussed over them for a while, but a baby can only do so much for so long for five-and seven-year-olds. Older boys, like me, can spend all day just watching, fully entertained.

"C'mon, Sammy," Joey said. "Let's go." They were out the door and onto their bikes.

The boys are outside playing now. Patty and Tommy are upstairs sleeping. And I'm just happy to be here.

Tommy's only two days old, but he's already had an impact on how I view baseball. He's one more reason it may be time to walk away from baseball at the end of this year.

Saturday, July 21
Bryan, Ohio

I called Joe Kerrigan in Nashville this morning. I was hoping he'd say he didn't need me.

"We're really hurtin', Fire," he said. "The afternoon game is the one I'm worried about, so if you could get here in time for that one, I'd appreciate it. Think you can make it?"

"Sure." What else was I going to say?

"Want me to get a flight for you?"

"No, I'll take care of it," I said, being the consummate professional that I am. I hung up and bit my lip. I then went upstairs and broke the news to Patty. We let off steam for about five minutes. "I didn't *have* to drive to Indy and pitch that stupid game for them two days ago," I said. "I'm so tired of this crap. What's *one* day? I know they're short on arms right now, but it's not like we're in a pennant race or anything."

Patty just sat on the bed and said, "I know, I know." I called the travel agent and got a flight out of Toledo into Nashville via two hours in Chicago. We complained some more, and then I went to pick up the ticket.

By the time I got back home, I felt a little better. Before the season started, I promised myself I'd do everything I possibly could to get back to the major leagues, and, thus far, I have. If I were to neglect Joe's request, I'd be breaking that promise. Even if I showed up, but had a chip on my shoulder and let it affect me on the mound, I'd be letting myself down. I gave myself a pep talk and tried my best to right my wrong attitude. Now that I've settled down, I realize that baseball itself really wasn't what angered me; it was the inconvenience that's been put on others. Patty is still recovering and could use my help around the house for another day. Joey and Sammy are usually willing to lend a hand, but it's often a frenzied ordeal. There are so many things they simply can't do. Someone will have to drive me to the airport in Toledo tomorrow morning. Some other lucky person will get to drive my car to Indy for me, and that'll have to be as soon as possible because the team will bus the five hours back to Indy after tomorrow night's game in Nashville.

Of course, yet another car will have to accompany mine so that both parties can return to Bryan. I haven't talked to my parents yet about the predicament, but I'll venture to say they'll again bail us out. They'll say, "I don't mind," or "We don't have anything else to do."

I mind.

Still, I resolved to not let this spoil my last day at home. I played with the boys outside. I even ran a few miles while they rode their bikes beside me. They got "totally" soaked while riding through "awesome" mud puddles. We ended our day by ordering pizza and watching a movie upstairs in our bedroom. We watched *Look Who's Talking* because the boys thought Tommy would like it. Of course, if you've ever watched a movie in a bed with your spouse, two little boys, and a baby (and I don't exactly recommend it, at least not if seeing the movie is your prime objective), then you know how little we saw. It was more like *Look Who's Watching*.

Sunday, July 22
Indianapolis

It's been a long day. I woke up early this morning and did some last-minute errands around the house for Patty. I showered, did some reading, and packed a few things for my trip to Nashville. Everybody was asleep so I walked around the bedrooms and said good-byes, more to myself than to my family. Patty woke up and we talked for a couple minutes. I heard my parents pull in the driveway, and I had to go. I took one last look at Tommy in his little crib. It takes a resilient heart to walk away from that.

We drove to Toledo and I got on a plane for Chicago, endured a three-hour layover, and hopped on another plane for Nashville. I took a cab straight to the park and arrived during the second inning of the afternoon game. I put my contacts in, my uniform on, and went to the bullpen.

The first thing I noticed was that we had another reliever. That made it tougher yet to believe that I really needed to be here, but I swallowed my anger and got involved with the typical bench-jockeying, trying to muster some enthusiasm for a long and boring 10–6 loss.

We now had two and a half more hours before the start of the second game. I went up to the Stadium Club here and had a bite to eat. I came back to our clubhouse, which was throbbing with some loud rap music. I put on my headphones, turned up the volume to where it smothered the opposition, grabbed a couple cups of coffee, and curled up inside my locker. It was even less relaxing than it sounds.

The second game went quicker. Nashville was ahead 2–1 in the eighth when we pinch-hit for our starting pitcher, Scott Anderson. I pitched the bottom of the eighth and had a three-up, three-down inning. We rallied to tie it in the ninth, and then they pinch-hit for me. We lost it in the bottom of the ninth, 3–2. This doubleheader was typical of our season.

The night was far from over, though. We were given an hour before the bus was to leave for Indy. The players get twenty-two of the seats on the bus—and tonight there were twenty-three players. In situations like that, first-year players usually have to share a seat. Instead, Dwight Lowry and I, who have more time in the big leagues than anyone here, sat together for the five-hour return trip. We could have forced the issue if

152

we wanted to, but we went with the flow, which was easy to do, since he and I enjoy each other's company.

We pulled into Indy at 3:45 A.M. Dwight called a cab to take us to our apartment complex. I got home at four-thirty and checked on my parents, in my bedroom, to make sure they were safe and sound. What a role reversal *this* is, I thought. I wonder how many times my mom checked to see if *I* was in during the middle of the night when I was a younger, more rebellious sort.

It's now 6 A.M. and I'm beat. I'll get up with my parents in a couple hours, have breakfast with them (decaf coffee this time), see them off as they head back to Bryan, and hibernate until I have to get up. Pitchers have early work at four-thirty today.

Monday, July 23
Indianapolis

The pitchers bunted for an hour today. The first half was off a pitching machine—always more difficult than a human because there's no arm motion to pick up the ball from. The primary advantage of machines is that they save a coach or manager from throwing. They're also supposed to be able to pump strikes consistently to the hitters. Ours cannot, and when Joe could no longer tolerate the machine's imperfection, he unplugged it and began throwing to us himself. He was at a rather close distance from us. This insured both accuracy for him and makeshift velocity for us. He drilled me right in the middle of my chest.

Howard was already bunting when we first assembled and was asked to continue after the rest of us were dismissed. His locker is now next to mine and when he came into the clubhouse ten minutes later, he was agitated by the extra work. "Why is it always me? When I mess up, I'm out there early all by myself the next day. When somebody else messes up, we're all out there and I *still* have to do more than anybody."

153

"You should know why," I said.

He nodded, either in recognition of his situation or in anticipation of what he knew I was going to say.

"I know it's hard sometimes," I said, "but you've gotta look at it from a positive angle. You're not asked to do more as a punishment. You're asked because Montreal wants to be able to expect more out of you. You're actually very fortunate. Try and look at it that way."

"I know," he said, and he smiled. "It still pisses me off sometimes."

While our team was still gathered in the clubhouse, ESPN did a follow-up on the first-round draft pick of the Oakland A's, some Texas kid named Todd Van Poppel, who signed a $1.3 million contract out of high school. As the young phenom's first start in A-ball was relived, the radio was shut off, guys put down their magazines, and the card game was put on hold. The kid went three innings, we learned, allowed but one hit ("an infield hit at that"), walked three and struck out *five*. "And his fastball was clocked in the low 90's!"

Such a strong initial outing prompted ESPN commentator Charlie Steiner to deduct, "It looks as though Oakland may have got its money's worth."

The clubhouse responded with a collective howl and several abusive one-liners, "I wish he'd gotten his tits lit!" yelled one of our younger pitchers.

There's a reason why guys here take an interest in that kid. A lot of people here feel they've been kicked around throughout their careers, and people who've been kicked around don't react kindly when they see handouts to others, either with money or opportunity. That kid serves as a reminder of everything most guys here never had. Maybe Oakland *will* get its money's worth. Maybe he will be *that* good. But people sitting here see him as a kid who's got a road paved straight to the big leagues, while they fight to keep their jobs and stay one step ahead of the competition and politics of their own circumstances.

Very early on, players recognize the "haves" and the "have-nots." This can be reversed, but that's a long, meandering path, not a paved road.

For Charlie Steiner to see so much in just three innings is absurd. That doesn't even deserve comment.

Tuesday, July 24
Indianapolis

I woke up this morning, read and prayed, made a pot of coffee, and turned on CNN, just like every morning. The sports segment came on, and after the previous night's scores were covered, they did a feature on home-run hitters. They billed the longball as the most exciting aspect of the game. I would have to agree, although I don't often view it as "exciting" from my place on the field.

Several power hitters were interviewed and all agreed that they enjoyed hitting dingers. The story concluded, or should I say climaxed, with an intimate chat with Jose Canseco. Fortunately, I'd already finished my breakfast.

"When I'm circling the bases," he said, "you can hear a pin drop. People in the stands are wondering how does he do that? What's this guy made of?"

Not once in my life have I wondered what he's made of. Sometimes, though, I wonder what he's thinking of.

As soon as I got to the park, Joe called me into Tim's office. "We're making a change," Joe said. "You're starting the first game in Buffalo, and you'll stay in the rotation. We're going to put Rojas in the pen. Keep it under your hat because we're not going to tell Mel until after the game tonight."

I was happy to hear it and gave an affirmative nod to Scott when I got back to my locker. He could have guessed what was said. Earlier in the year, when I was put in the pen, it was to make room for Chris Nabholz in the rotation. That's not to be confused with what's going on now. Mel isn't being made a reliever to make room for me. He's been throwing more strikes lately and it's been Montreal's intention all along to make him a reliever.

Our newest member of the team, reliever Yorkie Perez, is already out with an injury. It seems that whatever was hanging from his gold necklace flew up in his face and struck him in the eye. It could have been real serious. Some of the things guys dangle around their necks could give them bloody noses.

Yorkie's been told by the doctor to wear sunglasses, and it just looks strange to see him sitting in the dugout at 10 P.M. with shades on.

Wednesday, July 25
Indianapolis

Since Tommy's birth, Patty and I have received many congratulatory cards. We also have many friends both at home and here in Indy who have personally wished us well, and we're truly appreciative of everyone's support. More often than not, people will write or say something like, "Only six more and you'll have your own baseball team," or "I know *you* wanted another boy, Steve." We know it's just small talk. An orchestra conductor, no doubt, hears much the same thing on the birth of his "future violinist."

Still, there's some sort of assumption made that Patty and I would draw a lot of pleasure from raising athletes. I'm sure we would, and to some degree already have. The key word in that sentence is "raising," not "athletes." I can't say that I could care less what my sons do, and I certainly won't discourage athletics, but I won't be disappointed if their interests and abilities take them elsewhere.

There are those hard-line weekend-warrior athletes who are sincere when they wish me luck in "training" my boys. During the summer, this species can be observed playing softball decorated with sweatbands, batting gloves, and knee braces. I see them back in Bryan, pushing their sons and daughters beyond the kids' capabilities. Whose benefit is that for?

If our boys want to play baseball when they grow up, that's fine by us, and we'll help them in every way we can. That same loving concern would also apply to whatever else they dream of. We may not be able to offer as much advice in other fields, but it's not *our* lives that are being molded.

Baseball has bounced me around for many years. I've got as much right to complain as anybody I know in this game. I get tired of it, I get pissed off at it, and sometimes I want nothing to do with it. One day I feel I'm on top of the world, and the next I don't know which way is up. It messes with my family, doesn't promote consistency of life-style, constantly humbles me, and doesn't pay me all that much for the headaches. There are guys on this team who could tell you how many days are left in the season, just like a kid anxious to get out of school for the summer. Would I wish all this on my children? Only if it's what *they* wish. And if it is, they'll go into it with their eyes open.

Thursday, July 26
Indianapolis

I went to the park early today to throw on the side in preparation for Sunday's start in Buffalo. It felt good to get an extended workout in with Joe. I also ran five miles after batting practice. As a reliever I obviously couldn't do that just before a game, so it had been a while since I'd pushed my legs like that.

Mel Rojas was called up by Montreal this afternoon. He'll be used as a reliever up there. Nobody here is real sure what happened in Montreal to make room for him. Somebody probably went on the disabled list. If it were a trade we'd have heard about it. Mel has been pitching well lately and, of all our re-

157

lievers, he's no doubt the most deserving. I suppose there could be an argument made in that he hasn't made an appearance out of the bullpen all year.

There must be some concern about his arm, though. Because of a sore shoulder, he was unable to pitch in his last scheduled start and had to be pushed back three days. He went four innings two days ago. Montreal is in a pennant race and some may feel it would be to their advantage to go with some experience under those circumstances. Mel has never pitched in the big leagues. While his numbers are respectable here, I wouldn't trade mine for his.

What's done is done. I can't worry about what Montreal does. I'm not being ridiculously passive. I've just been around long enough to know how systems work. Montreal could easily justify Mel over me. He's several years younger, which could mean several more years of service. He strikes out more people than I do. Most importantly, they're familiar with Mel. He was brought up through this organization. They've had plans for him for a couple years now, as well they should. He has a strong arm, consistently throwing around 90. Montreal *could* justify the move. They don't have to, though. They're in the business of making decisions and I'm really nothing more than a hired hand—a hired arm, really. It's not our place as players to question organizational moves, although we all do. It's not within our rights to be critical of transactions, and the people who are responsible for them, but we often are. The farther away a player is from prospect status, however, the more he understands the conditions that are beyond his control.

Friday, July 27
Indianapolis

I received a message to call John Boles in Montreal today. "Fire, I'll get right to the point," he said, cordial yet straightforward, as always. "It's that time of year where I've got to put together my coaching staff for next season. I don't know what your plans are for next year. I don't know if you want to pitch again, stay in the game as a coach, or get out of baseball completely and get a nine-to-five. If you still want to pitch, that's great, but you can't be guaranteed a spot on Indy's roster next spring. There's too many kids with good arms in this organization."

"I'm not pitching for anybody here anyway, am I?"

"No," he said. "You're not. When Dave Schmidt went on the disabled list here, I thought to myself that maybe this is Fire's chance, but they went with Rojas. I'll be honest with you, Fire—it's just not going to happen. If they needed another pitcher up here, or even if they needed a couple more, it's not going to be you. I don't have to explain all this stuff to you. You know what goes on."

"I know, John," I said. "I don't have any doubts that if I pitched next year I'd pitch as well or better than I am this year. The same for a few years after that. But it's not really to anybody's benefit anymore."

"You're right," John said. "I look at you and I think, how long can this guy beat his head against the wall? The time is going to come when *you* have to take the ball out of your hand."

"I know."

"It's your decision, Fire. What *I'd* like to see you do is stay in the game as a pitching coach, and I informed everybody at today's meeting that I was going to offer you that job. Think about it for a week or ten days and give me a call back. You'd make a great pitching coach. I'm telling you, you'd spend more time in the big leagues as a pitching coach than you ever did or would as a player. Let me give you some advice, though. If you're still thinking about whether you want to do it or not after a week, don't do it."

Even though I'm painfully aware of what goes on, it still hurts to hear someone like John tell me it won't happen for me. It's almost like the final nail in the coffin. Still, there's only another month left in our season, and it'd be senseless for me to abandon my work ethic because John gave me some discouraging news, which really isn't news to me anyway. Just as there are no true guarantees that I'd make a great pitching coach, there's also nothing absolute denying my return to the big leagues as a player. I'm sure it's close to impossible, but it's up to me to decide which word I'll dwell on, "close" or "impossible."

However dim the light is at the end of the tunnel, I still need the direction it offers, or else I'm traveling aimlessly. Besides, what's another month? Anybody who has been at the same job for twelve or thirteen years can recall instances where they second-guessed themselves. I certainly have my share of those past mistakes. I'm not ever going to look back and question the effort I put forth in my final year, though, whether that year is this one or ten years from now.

Saturday, July 28
Indianapolis

I talked John's offer over with Patty today. It's a discussion we've had before, so it only lasted a couple minutes. Over the past several years, I've been approached by a few people about coaching jobs, so Patty and I have known for some time now that it's a possibility. We've never liked the idea much.

The number one drawback to baseball for me is the separation. What have I done to alleviate that if I stay on as a coach? It's tough on a family and it would only be tougher if I were a coach. The travel is tied to the separation, but is at the same time a separate complaint. I would be doing all those bus trips again and that does not appeal to me at all. And while I would consider myself able to get along with people, the thought of dealing with a lot of guys in their late teens or early twenties doesn't appeal to me, especially if they're athletes. That may sound very aloof, but I have a lot of hang-ups about "athletic" egos and I could visualize them getting in the way of teaching. That should in no way be interpreted as me placing myself above other people. It is just an opinion that could definitely hinder my ability to coach. There's no way I should ever be a professional coach if I have these reservations. It wouldn't be right for the organization or myself.

Still, if I were to be a coach, Montreal is the club I'd want to be affiliated with, and as I told John on the phone, I'm honored to have been asked. I think the philosophy on pitching that's taught throughout this organization is great. Looking back, I wish I'd been brought up in an organization like this. I don't want my sons to ever look back, though, and wish they'd been brought up with Dad around a little more.

I'm turning the job down. It's not a difficult decision.

Sunday, July 29
Buffalo

Before I got dressed for tonight's game, I went into the manager's office. Tim, Joe, and Gomer were all there, and I told them about my conversation with John Boles. "John's always been honest with me, and I've always respected him for it. He told me it isn't going to happen for me here as a player. What he'd like me to do is coach and he offered me a job in the organization for next year."

Tim smiled. "He told me months ago he planned on asking you. We've known that for a long time here, Fire."

"Well, as a player," I said, "it messes with me sometimes to feel I'm not pitching for any particular reason, know what I mean?"

They all nodded.

"In baseball, you never know," Joe said. "Let's just see how your last six or seven starts go, Fire."

I pitched well tonight. I went seven innings and allowed two runs, one earned, before being lifted for a pinch hitter. I gave up four hits, walked none, and struck out two. I threw only seventy pitches. I also got beat 2–1 again.

I haven't written much about the team lately because there's

161

not much to write about. I've never been associated with a team that has defensive breakdowns like this one. I don't mention that only because of the three errors tonight (although I admit that the errors served as a reminder). I have no idea how far out of first place we are, but I'm sure it's too far for this team to make up in a month. That's a pretty negative statement for someone who claims to be an optimist. Either there's a contradiction in my character, or we really are that bad.

Monday, July 30
Buffalo

Howard had another rocky outing tonight, giving up six hits and four runs in a 4–2 loss to Buffalo. He took the loss, which drops his record to 6–8.

I've played long enough to come full circle with baseball. I've been cast in every role I can think of in this game—including that of "prospect." I was never as highly regarded anywhere as Howard Farmer is here, but I was nevertheless seen as an up-and-comer.

As I mentioned earlier, I feel '84 was a season for me much like this season is for Howard Farmer. I had a great spring training and was sent out on the last day when a trade fell through. Instead of going down to Portland and doing what I needed to get back up, I pitched with one eye in Portland and the other in Philadelphia. I knew I was so close to being there and I was too anxious—not eager; *anxious*—to get back. It got so bad that I had to be taken out of the rotation by manager Lee Elia. "I don't know what else we can do," Elia said. "Maybe you'll throw the ball better out of the pen."

I did. It was the first time I'd ever relieved and once I got used to it, I pitched well. It even got to the point where I liked it—I was eventually called up to the Phillies. When I reported, pitching coach Claude Osteen came up and asked, "What happened to you the first part of the year?"

162

"I don't know," I said, which was the truth. It took me years to figure out what I'd done wrong. "But everything came back together when I went to the pen."

"Yeah," Osteen said. "That's what we've heard. I'm glad you're here now."

I pitched 5⅓ innings for the Phillies; shortly after the season ended, they released me. That was the first time I'd ever been released. I felt like I'd flunked a class or something.

Younger players look at releases that way. They take them too personally. A more experienced player thinks, "Okay, fine. I'll call my agent and see who else wants me."

I had no trouble finding other teams that wanted me. I chose the Chicago White Sox for '85. Once again, I came close to making the team in spring training. I was sent to Buffalo and pitched solid baseball. I was called up after a couple months and some management guy in a sport coat told me to go ahead and get an apartment in Chicago. "You're going to stay here," he said. "No problem."

I pitched seven innings in just over a month—not seven of my best innings, either.

Tony LaRussa, then the Sox manager, called me into his office. "We're going to send you back down," he said. "But I want you to know we're partially to blame for what happened here. We didn't use you as often as we should have to keep you on top of your game. I feel bad about it, but we have to get somebody here who's better able to contribute."

My first response was to place the blame on LaRussa. He even *told* me it wasn't my fault! But as time passed, and my insecurity passed as well, I took his remarks the way he meant them. Sure, he might have used me better. I might have pitched better, too. I returned to Buffalo and finished out the season third in the league in ERA.

My manager in Buffalo was John Boles. We talked at the end of the season, and we both felt the White Sox might still be the right organization for me.

Soon after that, I was released again.

August

Wednesday, August 1
Syracuse

I threw on the side today; my arm feels as strong as it has at any time in my career. The injury scare I had a few weeks ago, when I was afraid I'd reinjured my pectoralis major, seems to have passed.

That injury was really the least of my problems back in '86, though. I had offers from Seattle and Montreal that year. I've often wondered what would have happened had I gone the other way then. Most players—most people—sometimes tie themselves into knots about the career road not taken. Some have more roads to fret about than others.

I went to spring training with Seattle in Tempe, Arizona, and made a fine showing. As camp came to a close, I was sent to Triple-A Calgary, but I got recalled before I ever left Arizona. I spent a week with the Mariners before being optioned back down. In that week, I never came close to getting in a game. I was only a warm body, along for the ride until another player came off the disabled list. I reported to Calgary and all those fun Pacific Coast League hitters' parks again. I pitched well and worked hard. I really sensed I was with an organization that could use me.

Just twenty-nine games into the season, though, Seattle made a managerial change. The new skipper was none other than Dick Williams. Ross Grimsley, my pitching coach in Calgary, had played under Williams back in Montreal. Ross felt the same way about the guy as I did.

Still, I continued to pitch well and was called up in early June. I was used sparingly in relief and, at the All-Star break, I was 2–0 with the lowest ERA on the team. After the break, I returned to Seattle and was told I'd be returning to Calgary.

For me to say I couldn't believe it would just show that I was a slow learner. I believed it. I wasn't happy with it, but I'd been around long enough to see stuff like that happen. In this instance, the Mariners had decided that a higher-priced arm was healthy. Karl Best was *supposed* to pitch in Seattle, and when he came off the DL, somebody had to go.

My attitude stunk for a week or so, but I rebounded and pitched some strong games for Calgary. A month later, Seattle recalled me for the third time. I met the team in Anaheim and was told the team was going with a four-man rotation—and I'd be one of the four. I'd have my first start against Oakland a few days later.

I faced nine men in three innings. During the third, though, I ripped part of the nail off my middle finger, and I started bleeding all over the ball. Maybe it was caused by extra adrenaline, or maybe the seams on the balls were higher than on the balls I'd been used to, like what happened this year to Ben McDonald. The trainer put some gluelike substance over my finger to stop the bleeding. I went out for the fourth and faced two hitters. I walked the first guy and hit the second one. I had no feel for the ball and, as a result, had no clue where it was going. Dick Williams and the trainer came out to the mound and determined that I'd had enough. I was dejected, but positive I'd be ready for my next start.

It never came. The next day, Williams decided to go back to a five-man rotation, and I wasn't in it. How could I, in one day's time, pitch three shutout innings and go from being included in a *four*-man rotation to being excluded from a five-man?

Because I got hurt? The injury was a fluke and as mild as they come; I assured the trainer I'd be all right. Because I wasn't good enough? Check out the stats of the '86 Mariners pitching staff and tell me I wasn't good enough; there wasn't a starting pitcher on that team with an ERA under 4.30.

We were in last place and everybody knew that's where we'd wind up. I was again sent to the pen, where I was used sparingly. I was up with Seattle most of the year and pitched a total of ten games and twenty-one innings. During a game with two weeks left in the season, I was told to get ready, and a half-dozen pitches later, I felt something in my armpit give way. I finished the season sitting in the bullpen, unable to throw. It wasn't much of an adjustment.

We finished the season in Cleveland that year, which is only a four-hour drive from Bryan. I can remember showering as quickly as I could, eager to get out of there. I'd spent the majority of the year in the big leagues, and yet I was more anxious for that season to get over than any I can recall. I hustled out to our car, where Patty and the boys were waiting, and drove home. Not a word was spoken about baseball, not even from Joey. Patty must have advised him against it beforehand.

My agents spent the winter of '86 trying to get my release from Seattle. We'd anticipated no difficulty in getting away. Why would they want to hang on to me? But hang on to me they did. "Steve is going to be an integral part of our staff in '87," Mariners officials kept saying. To them I represented an insurance policy in case a rash of injuries broke out.

For all intents and purposes, that's what I've been ever since.

Thursday, August 2
Syracuse

Every time I come to Syracuse, it's hard for me not to think about the few weeks I pitched here back in 1987, the year my baseball life fell apart. When spring training rolled around that year, I was still a Mariner. The coaching staff insisted I change my windup and, company man that I am, I tried to comply. I don't have anything against trying what a pitching coach asks me, and I've been delighted this year with the adjustments Joe Kerrigan's helped me make in my delivery. But you don't drastically alter a man's delivery while he's scrambling to make a team.

A few weeks into camp, I was released.

That's what I'd wanted—six months earlier. Halfway through spring training is no time to be an unemployed ballplayer. For fringe players, spring training is a time for subtraction, not addition. What organization needs or wants a journeyman righthanded pitcher with marginal stuff halfway through spring training, when they're trying to slim down their rosters? None.

My family and I stayed out in Arizona until the spring-training period was over. No one called me. I was ready to get on with my life without baseball. We then packed our belongings and drove back to Ohio.

The day we made it back to Bryan, I got a call from Toronto. They asked me if I'd be interested in filling out the roster for their Triple-A team here in Syracuse. I accepted. They had some injured arms and I knew, going in, what my role would be. I sat in their bullpen for a few weeks and got into ten games, times when Syracuse had no other choice. When the injured pitchers got healthy, I was released. I should have been released. *I'd* have released me. I was closer to the loony bin than to Toronto, and I'd pitched hideously.

I came home and wasted the rest of the summer. I halfheartedly looked for jobs and played softball for my father-in-law's restaurant in the Bryan summer industrial league. I don't know what my problem was, but I had one. Maybe I thought I deserved some extended rest and relaxation after "all I'd been through." More than likely, I was just feeling sorry for myself. It was the darkest period of my life. Baseball had little to do with it. I didn't miss baseball. I was wandering aimlessly and taking my family with me. It was an extremely pitiful effort on my part in making an adjustment.

Just about when I was beginning to pick myself up, John Boles called. He was with the Royals then, and he asked me if I wanted to pitch again in '88. It caught me totally off guard. I may have had some apprehension about my future, but I was positive that baseball was a thing of the past. I didn't know what to say . . . for a few minutes anyway.

Patty and I talked it over and I agreed to the terms, and I was back in baseball. Royally.

Whatever I lost in experience that summer, whatever I lost off of and never regained on my fastball, I more than made up for in the appreciation I gained. I thank God for John Boles and the second life he gave me in this game. Whatever happens this year, and whatever I write here in this journal, please remember that underneath all my day-to-day worries is a feeling of gratitude that I learned in a season that never was.

Friday, August 3
Syracuse

I pitched well again tonight, although pitching at all tonight may have been the worst thing that's happened to me all year. I got a no-decision that figured heavily in another, more significant decision.

I went seven innings and didn't allow any runs. I gave up two hits, walked two, and struck out six. I would have liked to pitch more, but my arm was gassed. I had just over a hundred pitches, which normally wouldn't stop me. However, I threw over forty sliders tonight and when I have a good one, it takes a lot out of my arm. In the fifth inning, Syracuse led off with a double against me and, for the next four batters, I threw all sliders except for a couple of fastballs. I walked one of them and struck out the other three, so the strategy worked, but my arm paid the price. I had nothing left in the seventh. I came out with a 1–0 lead.

Syracuse scored twice off our relievers to pull out the win, 2–1. It's my third consecutive start that we've lost 2–1. I didn't absorb the loss this time, but that doesn't matter anymore. Whether I'm 7–9 or 8–9 doesn't make a whole lot of difference. It's obvious that I'm not going to rack up a ton of wins this season. Our yearlong slump is bigger than any of us.

We bused to Rochester after the game. Scott and I got settled and were just about to turn out the lights when the phone rang.

It was Joe. "I want you two down in the lobby right away."

It was 1:30 A.M. Scott and I were both whipped. We complained to each other, but we went, of course, trying on our way down to figure out what Joe needed. Our best guess was that he wanted to talk to a couple of the more experienced players and see if we had any ideas that would help our club.

Guess again.

Scott and I found Joe and Tim in the hotel bar. Tim didn't keep us in suspense. "Scott," he said, "you're going to Montreal. They need a pitcher for tomorrow's game in Chicago and they wanted one of you two."

Tim took a drink. Joe sat in silence. Scott and I took neither a drink nor a seat.

"Montreal has Gross to start the game," Tim said, "and Burke in relief and that's it. All the other relievers have been used too much the last couple days. We don't know what they're doing to make room for you on the roster or anything. They just want you there tomorrow."

Then Tim turned to me. "Fire, I wanted you here so you'd understand why it couldn't be you. They wanted to know who'd pitched for us tonight and I told them you went seven innings. There's no way they could use you tomorrow. It's just the way it's worked out."

"That's understandable," I said. I didn't like it, but at this stage in my career, I've come to expect it. I really did understand it. And I really did appreciate Tim telling me the news this way. No one had ever done anything like that for me before.

We all wished Scott the best and had a few laughs. On the way back up to our room, Scott said, "I feel great about going, but I feel kind of guilty, too. You're throwing the ball better."

I told him not to worry about it.

We both know that circumstances dictated the move. Scott's been pitching well, and there's really no reason for me to suggest that, even if we were both well rested, he wouldn't have gotten the call. Scott may only be up a few days. Then again, he might finish out the season in Montreal. When it comes to baseball and circumstances, one never knows.

Saturday, August 4
Bryan, Ohio

Scott and I got up this morning and boarded planes in different directions. Scott flew to Chicago and I came home for Tommy's baptism, which is to take place tomorrow. The team has two games remaining against Rochester before returning to Indianapolis on Monday. "I'm happy for you," I told Scott. "And I hope you stay up there, but I'm probably just as glad to be going home for the baptism."

"Yeah," he said. "I would be too. I wish I had that."

Ty Cobb, I thought, would roll over in his grave if he heard such a conversation. How could a baseball player be happy when he's *not* going to the big leagues, while another player, who is going to the big leagues, wishes for something more? I guess our priorities are messed up, huh?

My family was waiting for me at the Toledo Airport. We spent the rest of the day together. Joey, Sammy, and I goofed off between the chores I'd promised Patty I'd do. We closed the day with a heated game of Sorry, and Joey again came in fourth. He doesn't ever finish "last." He comes in "fourth" a lot, though, and just laughs about it.

We turned the television on to WGN to see if Scott was pitching. He wasn't, but we didn't have to wait long. Kevin Gross was getting hit hard, and Scott came in with the bases loaded, nobody out, and Andre Dawson at the plate.

Scott threw a pitch inside, but not inside enough. Dawson hit a ground ball down the third-base line, clearing the bases. Scott's final stats were three innings, one run, three hits, and a couple of strikeouts. Dawson hit the ball around the label of his bat, so it wasn't like he hit a terrible pitch. It's a game of inches.

Harry Caray and Steve Stone had little to say about Scott. Little good, anyway.

"And here's Scott Anderson," Stone said. "A career minor leaguer. He was up one time before with the Rangers and had an ERA of over nine!"

Harry recited Scott's yearly minor league won-lost records and said, "Sometimes you wonder what these minor league pitchers do that impresses their parent club."

I sat in my house, on my living room couch, shaking my head. The Expos needed a pitcher, and Scott deserved the promotion. He's worked hard all year. Of course, I'm biased. He's a good friend of mine. But I also know that nothing was handed to him.

Sometimes you do wonder.

Sunday, August 5
Bryan, Ohio

Today was perfect. Thomas John's baptism went well, and, after church, the entire family gathered for a cookout. Tommy's emergence has allowed me the rare opportunity to spend a few days at home away from baseball. I have nothing against my friends on the team, but it's great to escape that environment.

Almost all the people I've met in Indianapolis or in other cities are as a result of baseball. I know it's not uncommon to make new friends through one's occupation, and I'm thankful for all the people baseball has allowed me to meet. Still, baseball *is* the connection, and when you combine that with the infatuation many individuals have with the game, it leads to very one-sided discussions. *How's the arm? What's your record? Think you'll go up? How hard do you throw? You had a baby? Congratulations. What's your best pitch?*

I don't get annoyed by it because I know most people are genuinely curious and I realize it comes with the territory. In fact, someday I'll probably wish people still took such an interest in how I'm doing. I do get bored by baseball talk sometimes, though. With Patty, these conversations are even worse because usually it's *my* welfare people wonder about, not hers. Her identity gets lost in the shuffle.

Patty and I know full well we're not baseball's First Couple. My popularity is nothing in comparison to hundreds or thousands of others. We can only imagine what it must be like to be treated with superstar status. Even with my meager accomplishments, we get our fill of baseball-oriented friendships.

That may have been what made today so nice. We were with friends who could care less what I do for a living.

I'm not holding myself up above fans. I'm the same way to a certain degree. When I was with the Phillies, I sat for a few minutes at a small table in a hotel bar in Pittsburgh, talking with Bruce Springsteen. As much as I hate to admit it, I was taken by him. I'm no fan of his music and there's absolutely no reason I should have been impressed otherwise. There was that effortless communication, though, almost a kind of magnetism. Obviously, I can't relate to what it's like to be Bruce Springsteen or Cal Ripken. But it's refreshing to spend time with real friends.

Monday, August 6
Indianapolis

August has always been an uncomfortable month for me. From talking to other players over the years, I know I'm not alone in feeling the anxiety this time of year brings on. With a few scant weeks remaining in the minor league season, only a complete dope fails to recognize he'll soon be unemployed for the fall and winter months. You hear guys talking about their off-season plans—winter ball or goofing off, back to some office or factory. I'd wager that the vast majority of minor leaguers have no clue what they'll be doing with themselves shortly.

I'm more confused now than in any of my previous years. Earlier in the season—even as recently as a couple weeks ago—I was positive I'd be retiring from baseball. Now I'm not so sure. I'm pitching as well or better than I ever have, and as I wrote earlier, baseball is what I do best.

There are, though, some complications. I have one more mouth to feed. And if the separation from my loved ones is what I hate about this life-style, how can I justify being separated from one *more* loved one? My age is a factor, too. Do I look at myself as getting older or getting better? And what are my options? I've been asked if I'd like to play winter ball by another manager in our league. I don't want to. I've been offered a coaching job by the Expos. I don't want that either. I could possibly pitch in Italy next year, but I really can't see that working out. I have nothing waiting for me in Bryan except a dear family and a mortgaged house. I don't know whether I should look for something to get us through the winter or interview for an entirely different career. Either way, I'll have to start from scratch.

Last year, I was working within one week after I got home and continued to do so up until a few days before I left for spring training. Don't get me wrong: I'm no workaholic. I *had* to work that much. I only point that out to illustrate the urgency of my decision.

Maybe I'll get rocked in my last few starts. That might eliminate some avenues.

Wednesday, August 8
Indianapolis

I hurled my first shutout of the season tonight, against Buffalo. I gave up five hits, walked nobody, and struck out five. Only one runner got to second base, and we won 5–0. I threw 104 pitches and hit 90 miles per hour twice as often as I did in my last outing: two times.

Catcher Gil Reyes is having a love affair with my slider lately. I'm flattered, but he wears me out after six or seven innings. Then he makes fun of my fastball late in the game because I have nothing left. It's not really his fault. I could shake him off anytime I want and throw something else. Actually, we think a lot alike. That worries me.

After the game I talked to several reporters. They each asked me if I thought I'd get a shot with Montreal this year. "Your ERA is down to 2.38," they said. "You've pitched as well as anybody could the past month, and the Expos are struggling. Do you think you'll get a chance?"

What am I supposed to say? "The Expos are really stupid if they don't use me" or "Yeah, I can throw better than most of the guys up there"? All I say is, "Those decisions are out of my hands. I try to concentrate on what my job is here." That's all I *can* say. And it's the truth. Making some outrageous statement would serve no purpose.

As I was about to leave the clubhouse, one reporter came back up to me and told me Zane Smith had just been traded to Pittsburgh. That would leave Montreal with only four starters, which would seem to be an opportunity for me. But they have a couple relievers there who could easily go into the rotation. Believe it or not, I'm not worried about all this. I could sit here and theorize how I might fit into the picture. Maybe I could even convince myself that I *should* fit into the picture. Those are emotional roller coasters I got off a long time ago. All too often, disappointment follows anticipation. I wasn't always this way. It was a learned response. That doesn't mean I don't care. I just know how to handle it.

Thursday, August 9
Louisville

I went to the park early today so I could do some running. As I was changing clothes, pitcher Dan Gakeler came over to me. "You don't have to get dressed today," he said.

"What do you mean?"

"I heard John [trainer John Spinosa] making travel arrangements. I'll bet you're outta here."

"I doubt it," I said.

Just then Chris Nabholz stopped by on the way to his locker. "I'm leaving tomorrow," he said.

"Where are you going?" Dan asked, but I could have guessed.

"I got called up," Chris said.

We all congratulated him and wished him the best. Tim then got my attention and motioned for me to follow him outside. "Fire, I don't know what to tell you," Tim told me. "They said they want to groom a lefthanded starter. I told them how you were throwing. They said they're very much aware of it, and to make sure I told you that they know how good you're pitching." He shrugged. "You know, I don't want to press my opinions on you, but I don't think you should quit after this year. It'd be an easier decision for you if you were getting the crap kicked out of you every time, wouldn't it? I'll bet sometimes you wish you were."

"Yeah," I said. "It'd sure answer a lot of questions."

Then we started talking about our families and how hard it is to maintain them with baseball. I went back into the clubhouse, grabbed my Walkman, and went for a run.

It cracks me up that Tim was told to be sure and tell me that Montreal knows how well I'm doing. Should I be impressed that they know what's going on within their own organization? They're *supposed* to know. That's their job, just as it's my job to pitch.

Friday, August 10
Louisville

Chris Nabholz left this morning to join the Expos. Here's how our seasons compare:

	W—L	ERA	IP	H	BB	SO
Fireovid	8–9	2.38	136.0	130	30	67
Nabholz	0–6	4.83	63.1	66	28	44

I'm currently second in the league in ERA. I've allowed one earned run in my last twenty-nine innings. By all rights, you'd think it should be me that's promoted, right? Wrong. They *want* Chris to pitch in the big leagues. They asked me to be a coach next year. Montreal had ideas of me walking around next season with a clipboard in my hand, not a glove on it. That alone tells me how serious they are about me as a pitcher.

The issue isn't whether Chris, Howard, Scott, Mel, or anybody else who's been here and gone up throws well once they get to the big leagues. They're all quite capable of doing that, and I've pulled for every one of them. Chris may pitch a shutout for Montreal in the same game that I wouldn't have lasted two innings. Nobody can predict the outcomes. But my question is, how am I ever supposed to find out what I'd do? What do I need to do?

What I need to do is press on. I can't very well bad-mouth anybody or feel sorry for myself when I have no trouble understanding the situation. I don't like it. It's difficult to accept. And if you look solely at the numbers, it makes no sense. But I do understand yesterday's move. Chris represents the future. He's lefthanded, he's a prospect brought up through this organization, and his last two starts have been pretty good.

Where does all this leave me? I can't say for sure. I've worked hard all year, though, and it'd be silly for me to throw all that effort out the window with only a few weeks remaining in the season. Regardless of the level of pride they take in me, I still have my own.

Saturday, August 11
Louisville

I'm beginning to organize my thoughts for after the season—
or after the career, whichever the case may be in three weeks.
I had lunch today with a college buddy of mine who's tied into
the newspaper industry. Although his particular job deals
mainly with distribution, he's a friend of the company's
founder and owner. He's going to pass my name along, mention
this book, and tell him I'd enjoy writing in some capacity. It's
a huge operation and I'm sure they employ as well as turn down
numerous writers with more credentials and experience, but
what's there to lose? What if I follow through on this and they
turn me down? Rejection wouldn't exactly be something new
in my life.

I've made a list of people in Bryan I want to get in touch with
before the season ends, people who are in a position to hire or
maybe help point me in a direction. It's not likely that I'll have
any major breakthroughs over the phone, but I'll feel better
knowing I've at least made some preparations. I've sat down
with some Bryan executives before, and, quite naturally, they
ask, "What do you want to do?" or "How can you help this
company?" Even though I knew all these people on a personal
basis, I was tongue-tied the first few times I got these questions. Finally I combined telling the truth with selling myself.

Something like this: "You know who I am and you know
what I've done for the past decade. There are some transferable
qualities I'd bring from athletics that I think you'd find at-
tractive. I may not be able to tell you exactly what it is I can
do for you, but by the same token you can't tell me what I can't
do. I'm not stupid and I'm adaptable. I'm confident I could help
you."

All the above probably seems like strange material for a baseball book. It's what's on my mind, though. Although baseball
has provided unique opportunities over the years, it has never
afforded me the luxury of being able to disregard work outside

of the game. I could never hibernate over the winter until spring training rolled around, and now that I'm considering retirement, it's even more of an issue. Baseball will go on after I leave it. So will my workaday responsibilities.

Sunday, August 12
Indianapolis

Chris Nabholz pitched against the Phillies today and recorded his first major league victory. His performance will solidify his status in Montreal, as it well should. If Chris had gone up and been hit hard his first couple times out, it may have forced the Expos to consider somebody else. By picking up the win, Chris has reassured them, at least temporarily, that they made the right decision. Montreal won't feel the need to evaluate and project minor league pitchers with any sense of urgency if they're not forced to.

All the players here would like to believe their credentials are routinely discussed at great length in relation to how they could help the major league club. That's not how it works. Organizations keep a watchful eye on their prospects and only *seriously* speculate when a situation necessitates a move. It's just common sense. You don't fix it if it's not broke. There are enough concerns at the big league level already without concocting hypothetical call-ups.

We had a team picnic after our game today at the home of Hank Warren, the team's owner. It was the typical get-together with boosters and friends of the team invited. Patty and I usually stay at such events for a little while and then take off once we're convinced we've met the standards of a mandatory appearance. Today was different. As I was thanking Hank and his wife, Barbara, for their hospitality, the subject of fishing came up. I was marveling at their estate and Barbara pointed out how it was a shame there were no fisherman on the team because they have a lake on their property. I had Joey and Sammy under my arms at the time and they enthusiastically corrected Barbara. "We're fishermen!" they said. "We fish all the time!"

Where they came up with that is anyone's guess.

They won Barbara over, and, the next thing I knew, I was walking with Hank up the lane to their home, while Patty stayed behind and chatted with Barbara. The boys and I are going fishing sometime this homestand and Hank agreed to have lunch with me before the season ends. Aside from being a nice man, Hank also happens to be one of the most influential people in Indianapolis. It can't possibly hurt to share the vagueness of my future plans with him. I'm looking forward to meeting with him, and I owe it all to my boys, who've gone fishing a couple of times in their lives.

Montreal's predicament and mine are more parallel than I've been thinking. The Expos needed to make a move, considered their future, and made their decision. The problem is, we don't seem to be in each other's plans.

Monday, August 13
Indianapolis

It was chilly tonight at the park and my arm didn't like it at all. I could tell as soon as I began warming up that something wasn't right. I couldn't get loose. The arm didn't really hurt; it just ached all over. I started the game and during the first three innings it seemed to be getting better, but it went downhill in a hurry. We put heat on the back of my shoulder after the fourth. I couldn't throw a slider in the fifth and sixth innings, and Pawtucket jumped all over me in the sixth. I gave up four runs on two of the longest home runs I've ever served. They were bombs. On the night, I surrendered four runs in six innings of work, walked no one, and struck out five. I'd gone quite a while without giving up any runs, and I knew that streak would come to an end sooner or later. Four runs in one inning, though: that's an end and a half.

I don't really have any excuses. Joe asked me repeatedly if I wanted to continue and I kept saying, "I'll be all right." I can't willingly go into a set of circumstances and then blame my shortcomings on that.

Scott returned to us today. He was used only the one time in Chicago. He said he feels rusty and he doubts that Montreal has any plans for him the rest of the year. He's looking forward to becoming a free agent at the end of the season and signing with another team. By and large, we experienced Triple-A ballplayers are suckers for "the grass is always greener" theory. Some year when Scott's sitting in his rocking chair, he'll look back and think how wonderful it was that he pitched in the major leagues. It'll no doubt be a source of pleasure for him. It just seems strange to me that the same event that will be a future source of fond memories are a present source of bitter disappointment. It'd be stranger yet, though, if he were entirely content with what he's accomplished this season.

Tuesday, August 14
Indianapolis

This morning's paper had a nice article about my scoreless streak coming to an end. Joe said he knew I was in trouble right from the get-go. "He pitched on pure guts tonight," Tim was quoted as saying. Like everyone else, I enjoy hearing or reading positive things about myself. I don't dwell on any praise that comes my way, but it's always good to know my efforts are appreciated.

When I read Tim's quote this morning, though, all I could do was laugh. Tim knows why, too. He was just being complimentary. I no more pitched on "pure guts" last night than I pitched lefthanded. I continued to pitch because I had nothing to lose by doing so—and besides, I *was* getting people out. If I strained my arm or stretched my pectoralis major, what would happen? I'd be a little more stiff than usual the next couple days. Or if the soreness was more severe, which I don't think it is, I might have to be pushed back a day or two in the rotation. My staying in the game certainly didn't jeopardize the team. We're twenty games out and short on healthy arms. I also doubt whether Montreal would be concerned. Most importantly, this is the time of the season—as well as the stage of my career—where I'm not too worried about a few aches and pains.

I called Hank Warren this morning, much to my boys' delight. We're going fishing Thursday, and I'm having lunch with him next week. I think my best plan of attack in preparing for the future is to audition as though I'm completely convinced I'm finished with baseball. That's the safest and sanest mind-set to adopt. If I *am* finished, I'd like to be prepared for it. If I'm wrong, that'll be an easy adjustment.

I've pitched well enough this year to confuse me.

Wednesday, August 15
Indianapolis

John Boles is in town this homestand to observe the team. We sat together in the stands, and he shared some insights with me from a front-office point of view.

"Only four percent of kids drafted ever set foot in the major leagues," he said. "A good hitter is retired seventy percent of the time, and pitchers are only doing their jobs when they don't allow any runs. It's a negative game and the older a player gets, especially in the minor leagues, the more he becomes aware of that and it's easier for his personality or attitude to become negative. Some deal with it better than others."

He pointed to our dugout. "You see all those guys sitting down there? Every one of them thinks he's been screwed. They've all got sob stories and they all think they belong somewhere else. It's the nature of the Triple-A beast. You know what I wish for, Fire? I wish every single one of them could take two or three weeks after their careers are over, come up into the front office, and help make the decisions. Every decision that's made, somebody thinks he got screwed."

We also talked about my future a little bit. I told him about my plans to get together with Hank Warren here and later with Bob Rich, Jr., in Buffalo. "Those are two very good men to talk to," he said. Then baseball came up. "You know, Fire, it could still happen for you in this organization. I know I told you earlier it wasn't going to, but last night was the first time you've given up any runs since then. When the Zane Smith trade happened, and they needed a pitcher, they didn't know whether to call up Nabholz or Barnes [a lefthanded prospect in Double-A]. Rick Williams, Tim Johnson, Joe Kerrigan, and I all stepped in and said to forget about those two, that Fireovid should be brought up." He shrugged. "They were insistent that a lefthander be groomed."

"You don't think they'll call me up at the end of the year, do you?"

"I know it's been *recommended*."

"Aren't I a little old to get a pat-on-the-back-type call-up in September?"

"They wouldn't bring you up for that reason."

John Boles's name is synonymous with honesty. If he now says there's a chance, there's a chance. I presume that chance is slim, but I'm not under obligation to forecast my future here. The organization's opinion of me could change like the weather, but it shouldn't affect my mental approach toward my work. It may be a cliché, but all I can do is my best. I've got my responsibilities and they've got theirs.

Two nights ago I wrote that I didn't really care about any unnecessary risks with my arm. But suppose my arm feels the same when I take the mound in Buffalo three days from now. After what I learned from John tonight, I'm not so sure that I wouldn't take myself out of the game. An injured arm reduces my chances from slim to none.

Still, changing my outlook so abruptly makes me feel like a

hypocrite. If my only job here is to pitch and not be swayed by my guesses about Montreal's intentions, why should my outlook change based on a few words from John?

I guess this Triple-A beast is just thinking too much.

Thursday, August 16
Indianapolis

Scott stopped by the apartment early this morning to join us on our fishing expedition. The boys were excited beyond words. We went to a bait shop and bought some night crawlers, plus a few other novelties to fill up the boys' tackle box. When we got lost on the way to the lake, Joey in turn lost his patience. "We'd probably find the place," he said, "if you guys would quit talking all the time."

We finally located the lake and jumped into the rowboat. The next couple hours were not to be confused with the tranquil setting often associated with fishing. It surely left a lasting impression on Scott, who has no children yet and who was the only one of us who'd ever really fished. We were like (please forgive me) fish out of water.

We never stayed in one spot for more than fifteen minutes. Sammy barely kept his line in the water long enough for it to get wet. "Dad," he kept saying, "I'm going to rod it in now."

"Reel," I'd say.

We replaced dozens of poorly baited worms, generally got in each other's way, and caught one fish. Sammy hooked a "blue-bill," more commonly known as a bluegill. Joey was typically long on advice and short on knowledge. Scott kept everybody in order to the best of his ability. I spent a good chunk of time trying to extricate my bobber from a sycamore tree.

After we were done, we drove back to the apartment, where Patty had lunch waiting. I have little doubt that Sammy will become an ethical fisherman—someday. As he described his catch to Patty, the fish had already doubled in size. Scott met little Tommy and took off. Then it was time to load up the station wagon for Patty's return trip to Bryan. It's the time of the season when I send a lot of my belongings back with her.

Once that was accomplished, I was attacked by two boys who "more than anything" wanted to go to the ballpark and play around. There must have been some sort of misunderstanding on my part. This morning, I could have sworn they told me they wanted to go fishing "more than anything." But they talked me into going to the park and quickly changed from shorts into their uniforms.

We went to the yard, and I tried to wear them out but was forced to stop because of exhaustion. We horsed around until Patty came with the baby to pick them up. I hustled them into the clubhouse, where they each had a final chance to pee, and then I raced them out to the car. The pitchers had already started bunting, so we didn't have time for long good-byes. I gave all four of them a kiss and ran back to the field.

I stood waiting for my turn to bunt, around other guys but somehow alone. I just went from feeling like the ultimate dad, I thought, to feeling not like much of a dad at all. I know they're still my sons when we're apart. I wish I *felt* it more. More than anything.

Friday, August 17
Indianapolis

I found out today from a friend of a friend of a friend that another team would like to have me next year. Okay, fine. I'm not concerned about credibility in the link of acquaintances, but I do question the authority of the source of that information. Whether it came from a scout in the stands, another manager, or the owner of the franchise doesn't mean a whole lot to me without an understanding of who's involved in actually making decisions in that particular organization. No two organizations are structured the same. From one club to another, similar responsibilities may fall under different titles. Two "vice presidents in charge of operations" may have greatly contrasting roles. One may be an organizational pawn while the other is a mover and a shaker. I don't doubt that there's some interest in me; I've heard of a couple additional teams that have an eye on me as well. But I'm not going to hear anything now; no team would risk tampering charges pursuing me.

First of all, I'm undecided as to what I'll do next year, and secondly it's not the time to get all worked up about it anyway. Once the season is over, I'll find out which teams, if any, want me, try to find out who in the organization wants me, and, finally, attempt to decipher how much clout that person has. Then I'll decide if I'll do it again. It sounds much more systematic than I'm sure it'll be. Whatever outside-baseball considerations that surface will probably play as large a role in my decision as any inside-baseball stuff.

Tonight was the final game of the homestand. That could also mean it'd be the last time I'd be in contact with John Boles. After I showered and dressed, I was on my way into Tim's office to thank Boles again for everything he's done for me. Instead, he intercepted me in the clubhouse. "I'll see you later, Fire," he said.

"I don't know about that, John. I was just on my way in to thank you."

"Trust me," he said. "I'll see you later."

With that, we shook hands. "Okay," I said. I wouldn't go as far as calling John a prophet, but odds are I'll see him again.

Saturday, August 18
Buffalo

My arm felt much better tonight than the last time out. I was strong, but I didn't have my best slider to offer. It's not surprising and I'm not disturbed by it. The slider has been con-

188

sistently sharp for a couple months now and I've spotted it well. Some nights, though, a pitcher simply has better stuff than others. The secret is to keep the off nights to a minimum, and then learn how to battle when you don't have your good stuff.

I went six innings tonight before being lifted for a pinch hitter in the seventh. I gave up seven hits, walked one, and struck out five. Buffalo scored four runs off me, but only one or two of them were earned, depending on whether we were charged with three or four errors; I forgot to look. Over my last six starts, I've probably had more errors committed behind me than runs scored for me. In five of those six, we've only scored one run. I don't mention that for pity or to get down on my teammates. That's baseball. I might very well go out next time and get shelled for seven runs in five innings and pick up an 8–7 win. Naturally, I'd rather win, but so would everybody else on the team. We're all trying, and we're all falling short of what we'd like. It's a collective stench.

Chris Nabholz turned in a very solid performance against the Dodgers tonight. He belongs where he is and he's proven that to the Expos in all three of his major league starts. Do you think Montreal is the least bit disturbed right now that Chris was 0–6 here with a 4.83 ERA? They aren't and they shouldn't be. If a player takes full advantage of his big league opportunities, who cares about his minor league past?

Sunday, August 19
Buffalo

I had a spur-of-the-moment conversation with Joe this afternoon during a rain delay. He knows I have no definite plans for next year. I wasn't looking for anyone to inflate my ego or talk me into playing again. I just wanted some answers that might help me make a decision.

"I've thrown well enough to confuse me," I told Joe. "If I'd

189

been getting lit all season—or on the other hand, if I was in the big leagues now—it'd be an easy decision. I don't want to go about anything halfheartedly. I either want to leave the game and get on with something else or be committed to pitching again."

Joe nodded. "I know you do," he said. "My recommendation to Montreal was that they should call you up and take a look at you. I wrote in my report that you're a guy we should hold on to because teams don't win pennants with ten pitchers. They win them with fifteen or sixteen pitchers, and you could help them do that. I wrote that you could easily be that eleventh, twelfth, or thirteenth pitcher on the staff, a guy who could either start or relieve if called upon."

"What about being the tenth pitcher?"

"Yeah, that too."

"You know, for the past couple years," I said, "when the big league teams were carrying twenty-four guys on the roster, I always felt like the twenty-fifth man. Now they're carrying twenty-five again, and I'm pitching better than I ever have, and somehow I've become the twenty-sixth man."

Joe didn't say anything. There wasn't anything to say.

"So you think there's a possibility they could call me up," I said, "and keep me on the forty-man roster over the winter because I'd be a good insurance policy?"

"I have no idea," Joe said. "I guess it could be a possibility."

"Would I be crazy in thinking there's a chance I could come to spring training next year and be looked at in a somewhat serious manner? You know, not a courtesy invitee with the predetermined cut at the first available date?"

"It could happen."

Just then Tim walked through the door from his adjoining office. "I've been over there listening to you two," he said, "and I can tell you, Fire, that everything Joe said is true. We don't know what Montreal is going to do over the winter, but we've both suggested that they keep you. If you would have come in here three months ago and asked my opinion, I'd have said do what you want to do and wished you the best of luck. I can't say that now. Not the way you've been pitching. You're throwing too good to quit."

"Yeah, Fire," Joe said. "If you came in here looking for someone to talk you out of playing, you're not going to find him."

I thanked them for their time and saw my way out of the office. All of a sudden, I felt like a kid in grade school who scored well on a test, but wanted the teacher to further prove it by putting a pretty sticker at the top of the paper.

Monday, August 20
Buffalo

I was unable to meet with Bob Rich, Jr., while we were in town. He's been traveling across the country in an effort to promote major league baseball in Buffalo. I hope they land a franchise here. The fans are both enthusiastic and supportive. The Triple-A team here draws better than a half-dozen of the major league teams. It's a first-class operation, and I know it would only get better if Bob Rich's dream materialized. If Buffalo can consistently sell out football games at Rich Stadium, with the winters they endure, they deserve a chance to support a baseball team.

That's written, obviously, with more sentiment than anything else. I'm hoping that Bob will accompany his team to Indianapolis for the season finale, but I'm told it's doubtful. My disappointment at not getting together with Bob was more than made up for by a visit from my best friends from home. They're here taking in Niagara Falls, and it was wonderful to go out with them after tonight's game and kill a couple pots of coffee.

As I've mentioned before, the friendships I've made through baseball are special to me, too. I think what makes baseball-oriented relationships unique to me is that I not only observe but live with people as they go through extreme highs and lows. I learn more about a man when I see him under adverse

191

conditions. And I don't just get a glimpse of him at work with baseball. The itinerary insures that I'll see him off the field a fair share of the time, too. I can't help but run into him. We live together half the season. Nine-to-five people can escape from their frustrations—and their coworkers—at home, or at least hide them there. We can't do that. There are no weekends to retreat to, and there's an almost overwhelming amount of pressure felt to perform. Stress, admittedly, is a self-imposed problem, and some people handle it better than others. I work, eat, sleep, travel, and goof off with some guys who are walking time bombs. Others are pillars of strength.

I'm not slighting the pressure felt in the business world, but I've talked with dozens of guys now retired from the game who've replaced their uniforms with suits. Every single one of them has told me the pressure they feel now is nothing compared to what they experienced as a player. Whether that unscientific sampling is reliable, I don't know.

August typically finds baseball players worn out, especially those in the minor leagues. Our bodies are tired, we're tired of traveling, we're tired of losing, and as much as anything, we're tired of each other. There's a popular phrase in baseball I've heard in every previous season, a phrase I hear every day now: "Two more weeks until you can pick your own friends." It's the truth. I had a temporary break from the routine tonight with Bill and Deb. I'll see a lot more of them in a couple weeks.

Tuesday, August 21
Indianapolis

I woke up at 5 A.M. after a few hours of sleep, in time to shower and catch the bus to the airport in Buffalo. We arrived back in Indy around nine, and I took another bus to the stadium, where I'd left my car for the road trip. I went into the trainer's office and called Hank Warren. We'd planned to have lunch this noon, and I wanted to make sure we were still on. We agreed on a time and location. I gave Scott a ride home, went to my apartment, changed clothes, and drove off to meet with Hank. I jokingly told Scott in the car that I thought I'd like the place Hank picked to meet. It was called Woodstock. With my rock and roll background, I figured I'd feel right at home.

It turned out to be nothing like Max Yasgur's farm. It was a very old, very posh country club with fairways better manicured than the greens I occasionally play on. I found my way to the restaurant, where Hank was waiting for me.

We ordered and quickly involved ourselves with the future. I explained my situation both in and out of baseball and speculated on the possibilities within each realm. His advice was logical and offered with conviction. Somehow that didn't surprise me. "What's one more year in your life, Steve? I'd guess you have at least five years left in your arm. You're pitching as well as you ever have, and people from this organization want you back. Other clubs have interest in you, too."

"If I decided to pitch again next season," I said, "I don't think I'd have any difficulty finding a job."

"Exactly. I think you're being a bit hasty about your predicament."

"Yeah, but I wonder sometimes if I'm not just stalling the future. I see so much uncertainty there and maybe baseball is just a convenient way to avoid facing it for another year. I don't feel that way when I'm on the mound or while I'm doing the other work involved with it. But, still, I don't have much to show for the effort."

"Aw, sure you do," Hank scoffed. "You never know what doors will be opened to you once you retire from baseball. The point is *you* don't *have* to quit. Life will present enough problems as it is. Don't try to tackle those that are unnecessary."

We finished our lunch and he showed me around the club. He also wants me to meet a couple acquaintances of his over our next homestand.

Everything Hank said makes sense. His suggestion wasn't a new idea to me. It was just the one he voted in favor of. It'll all work itself out, I guess. There are certainly tougher decisions made every day than what I'm contemplating. How many grown men are fortunate enough to be able to decide whether they want to play baseball or not?

There are several thousand men in Saudi Arabia right now, engaged in their career of choice, who have *much* more at risk than I do.

Wednesday, August 22
Indianapolis

Patty and the boys drove down today. It was out of necessity as much as anything. This is only a three-day homestand, and, under normal conditions (if our family life even has such a thing), Patty'd probably choose against making the trip for such a short period. I'm moving out of the apartment in two days, though, and we have some stuff to haul back to Bryan.

Tommy is a moose. He changes so much every time I see him. I couldn't believe how he'd grown. Fortunately, he's a good baby. He sleeps through the night and remains peaceful (for the most part) when he's awake. He does take up a lot of Patty's time, though, and if that's not enough, the other two take turns driving her nuts.

I've been named "Player of the Game" a few times this season and have saved all the gift certificates awarded me. I told Patty I wanted to take her shopping today and maybe get her a jacket.

"Fine. I need a strait one," she said, laughing.

It's hard on her. Much harder than I realize. Her life will be as affected as mine by what I decide to do. If she so desires, she could put her foot down and say, "I've had enough of this. I don't want you to play anymore." She knows I'd quit if she felt that strongly about it. Instead, she remains supportive— not of baseball, but of me. Not all baseball wives can look at themselves in the mirror and say that. We talk about our future frequently these days. It's remarkable how she'll constantly use the words "you" and "we," rarely the word "I."

194

I'll bet she thinks I don't notice.
I do.

Thursday, August 23
Indianapolis

Patty and I spent the entire morning cleaning the apartment. We've done it so many times before that there isn't a great deal of communication needed. She does the areas that she does best, and I do likewise. She's kitchen and bathroom; I'm everything else. Our high standards of cleanliness are usually unappreciated. We leave all our apartments in better shape than what we found them in, but never come close to getting our full deposit back. There's not much we can do about it. We'll get a check from the apartment complex in a few weeks for the amount of our deposit, minus all expenses "needed" to clean up after us. They have players over a barrel because they know we're not going to drive or fly back and make an issue out of it.

Packing is a piece of cake for us. First of all Patty and I only use the bare necessities at our summer residences anymore; our days of renting U-Hauls are long gone. We have a couple boxes that house our seasonal belongings. We take them home, throw them in the attic, and forget about them until the following spring. Included are a rather inexpensive set of pots, pans, plates, cups, silverware, cheap towels, and sheets. We never decorate our apartments at all, so there are no pictures or furniture to take home. Besides, if we put a hole in the wall to hang a picture, the leasing personnel may decide that the entire apartment needs to be overhauled.

Another reason packing is so easy for us is experience. Patty and I have moved more than we care to think about. This is our tenth year together in baseball. Consider the packing and unpacking process that's involved with us. We start in Bryan, then spring training, then the season, with its multiple set-

195

tings, and finally Bryan again. That's a lot of moving. If only through sheer repetition, we're proficient enough at it now that it's no big deal.

Patty and I got done and dedicated the afternoon to our family. It was sort of like "scheduled bonding." We didn't do much except sit around the apartment and make sure the boys didn't touch the walls. It was the type of fun reserved for families. Before long the afternoon was spent, and it was time to go to the park.

I was sluggish all night. I went seven innings and gave up four runs on seven hits. I struck out four and didn't walk anybody. I may have had my best fastball of the year but for the second start in a row had no slider to speak of. We scored five runs in the second inning and held on to win 5–4. I hit a bases-loaded double to help our cause.

After the game, two or three reporters asked me the same question: "Do you think you'll go up?"

"I have no idea what's going to happen," I said. It's all I could say. "I have two starts remaining in the season and I plan on finishing up as strong as I can."

I got out of the clubhouse as fast as possible. Since we had no food in the apartment, the five of us went out for pizza. Then we rushed back and tucked the boys in bed. Tomorrow will be an early and busy day.

Friday, August 24
Tidewater

The following is a demographic breakdown of the players on this team:

    12 Whites
    5 Blacks
    4 Dominicans

1 Puerto Rican
1 Venezuelan
1 Indian
1 Filipino

With such various cultural backgrounds, it's no wonder there are differences of opinion with regard to dress, food, and even baseball itself. However, there's no better evidence of the contrasting styles than our musical tastes. All clubhouses have some sort of stereo on hand for the players' listening enjoyment. The problem is that what one guy finds enjoyable, another guy finds insufferable. It's a battle that's waged every day over the duration of the season. If I don't like what's on the radio, I verbally assault those who obviously have wooden ears. On those rare occasions when my tastes are met, my capacity to enjoy is directly proportional to my ability to block out the howls from the deaf majority. It's the same with everybody. They're equally entitled to their opinions. Even if they're wrong.

There's not much middle ground with rap. Guys either like it or hate it. For those of us who hate it, it's an easy target for insults.

Another camp is devoted to Latin music. At low decibel levels, I don't mind it. Of course, I don't understand the language, so all the lyrics sound the same. It is danceable stuff, especially for athletic Latins, admittedly the only type of Latinos I'm around. I can watch German Rivera or Johnny Paredes dance for a couple songs and laugh along with them. Then I want a change of pace.

We have some Top 40 listeners, too, white guys who have no real interest in or knowledge of music. "I hear this song all the time," these guys must (at least subconsciously) think. "It *must* be good. I *should* like it. I *do* like it." This music doesn't do a whole lot for most guys, but has the best chance of remaining on the airwaves because it doesn't offend many people. It's basically Muzak for aging children.

We have a couple of "good ol' boys" who like country music. I've been on teams where country was the dominant choice.

Those were long years. Actually I don't mind that stuff too much as long as it isn't another twangy eighteen-wheeler story. Eddie Dixon, nicknamed "Dixie," heads up our small group of country boys. Dixie doesn't try his luck at the radio very often. He knows he's overwhelmingly outnumbered.

There's always hard-rock fans, almost always younger white guys. I can handle it if it isn't too adolescent and trashy. The blacks and Latins, though, lash out at this stuff. They'll deride the guitar onslaught by making jokes about black-light posters, getting stoned, and other hippie terminology. Jim Davins is this team's biggest heavy-metal fan. When he's deeply committed to his cause, he sits by the blaster, smiling, turning up the volume a little more with each successive outrage.

In twelve years of pro ball, I've almost never come across ballplayers who love jazz or classical music. I mean *real* jazz, not the commercialized stuff. This doesn't speak well of the collective intelligence in the game, although I'm by no means as up on my Mozart or my Ellington as I wish I were.

When I get to the park, before I enter the clubhouse, I can tell who's already there, just by listening to what kind of music's on. I'm never really one of the guys who fights hard for control of the stereo. I get more amusement from watching guys inflicting their tastes on each other, with the inevitable ragging that follows, than I do from what finally plays.

Sunday, August 26
Tidewater

After I got to the park today I was sent to a hospital by trainer John Spinosa. I've had some internal pain, in my stomach and on the right side of my back. Today a rash broke out on the skin directly above where the pain is located. It took the physician about ten seconds to diagnose the problem. I have shingles. It feels like somebody took a baseball bat and laid a couple swings against my midsection. The rash is really nothing to worry about—I'm told. It attacks from within. Supposedly, it'll last two or three weeks and go away. I've already had it in a less severe stage for a week, so it shouldn't be around much longer.

I may not be able to pitch, especially since it's on my right side. If considerations are now being made about the September call-ups, the last thing I need is to be unable to throw. For all I know, the decisions may already have been finalized. But I can't afford to carry on under that assumption. Still, worrying isn't going to help. All I can do is take it easy, pray for the best, and take the medicine prescribed. I'm now on steroids, or I will be soon. The drugstores were all closed by the time I was finished at the hospital.

Right now I'm on a bus from Tidewater to Richmond, and I feel pretty rotten. The music and the chatter aren't very soothing, but I can't expect everybody to be quiet because I don't feel well. I just want to get to the motel and crawl in bed.

Monday, August 27
Tidewater

I received permission from Tim to stay back at the motel tonight instead of going to the park. I wouldn't do anything there except sit in the dugout and sweat, and the perspiration irritates the rash. I don't feel any worse today. In fact, if anything, the pain seems to have subsided some in the back. I think I'll be able to pitch tomorrow night.

This is an extremely rare day off. Players are almost always required to at least show up at the park, unless they're seriously ill. That's not the case with me. There's only a week left in the season. We're twenty-one games out of first, nobody benefits from my presence tonight, and I told Tim I'd be able to pitch tomorrow, so all things considered Tim decided to let me stay behind. I'll admit to feeling a little guilty, but not enough to ruin my brief vacation. This is probably how Joey feels when he's too sick to attend school, yet has no difficulty watching TV or playing with Legos.

Speaking of school, Joey and Sammy had their first day of a new year today. Sammy is entering kindergarten. He's awfully conscientious for his age, and Patty and I joke that he's been suffering from performance anxiety this week. Joey is now in second grade. He's just the opposite; he's confident his high school diploma and college acceptance letter are long overdue.

I can see the park all lit up from where I'm sitting in my room. I like the game a lot, but I don't think that's the cause of the smile on my face. In my weakened condition, I owe it to myself to write a letter, read a while, and maybe watch a movie.

Tuesday, August 28
Richmond

The shingles are evidently in a state of remission. I experienced only a tiny bit of discomfort tonight and tossed a two-hit shut-out. I walked two and struck out one in going the distance for our 3–0 win. Richmond sent twenty-nine batters to the plate, and only one man reached second base.

In all honesty I didn't feel as good as the stats would indicate, but my sinker was diving into righthanders all night. The slider was better than the past couple games, too, although it's still a right-to-left movement with not enough bite downward. Believe me, I'm not complaining. I'll take these results anytime. But neither am I being too critical of myself. I've felt much better and had far less to show for it. It's a funny game.

I drove in another run tonight as well. After the game, a Richmond reporter asked me how I approached hitting their ace, Paul Marak. I'd just thrown my best game of the season, and the first thing this writer wants to know about is my hitting. Everybody within earshot cracked up. I put on a dignified face and spoke directly into the tape recorder. "I have a very simple approach to hitting," I said. "If it's straight and I think it's a strike, I swing at it."

The home-plate umpire was tight tonight, especially early in the game. I have virtually no temper, but Patty has assured me over the years that I possess a glare which more than communicates any hostility. I guess the umpire had had enough of my staring at him in the fifth inning. It got to the point finally where he called a ball and I screamed at him, "Where?"

He yelled back, "Down!"

I responded with my glare.

Catcher Gil Reyes came out to the mound. "Fire, he told me to tell you he's tired of you making faces at him and that he's been giving you those pitches lately."

"That was a strike."

"Could have been low."

"Whose side are you on?" We both laughed and he headed back to the plate.

The umpire called a much better game from that point on. In fact, he gave me a couple strikes that were outside the zone. Some umpires really put the screws to you after a little spat. Others loosen up. I was lucky tonight. The whole problem could have been avoided, though, if he'd poked a couple holes in his mask a little sooner.

I have one start remaining in the season. It's hard to believe the season's almost over. Joe told me before the game that he still doesn't know who is going up to Montreal. I'd be foolish to have any attitude other than preparing for one final start. I could have my best years in baseball still ahead of me, but there's also a possibility that Sunday could be my last appearance on a mound.

Wednesday, August 29
Nashville

We got beat tonight, 6–1. The novelty of this particular loss was that I scored our run after being inserted in the game as a pinch runner. Howard Farmer started for us and had breezed through the first two innings. Then the rain came down. Howard rarely embarrasses himself at the plate and had just ripped a double with two outs in the top of the third when the umpire ordered the tarps back over the field. After an hour delay, play was resumed. Howard was no longer our pitcher; Tim and Joe obviously feared that, because of the delay, his arm may have stiffened up. That's a logical decision—even more logical when the party in question is a prospect. Howard *shouldn't* have continued.

When the action picked up again, I replaced Howard as the base runner at second and turned a routine RBI single by Eric Bullock into a bang-bang play at home, but scored nonetheless. Several of my teammates yelled words of discouragement while I clogged up the bases. It was fun, though, and I was given a large reception as I returned to our dugout. A couple guys asked me why Howard didn't run for himself. I wish I could have replied, "Because I'm faster." But by then, Howard was already out of the game and in the clubhouse. Not only that, the field was a sloppy mess and Howard's career isn't going to be jeopardized by unnecessary risks, whether it be by turning an ankle or a collision at home plate. Some of the jeers directed at me were pretty amusing. "Yeah, let's send the old mare out to run. If she gets hurt we can just shoot her."

Howard will be going up to the big leagues tomorrow or the next day. We got the news today that Montreal wants him up there now so he can be included on their playoff roster, should the Expos somehow win their division. Outfielders Rolando Roomes and Moises Alou will go up with him. It's possible that others could be promoted at the conclusion of our season in five days, but that's only speculation on my part. I'm certainly not counting on it.

Thursday, August 30
Nashville

I was told today that it's not likely any additional players will be called up after the season is over. It's not definite, but close to it.

Obviously, I have to wonder what it is they don't like about me. My age may not be working for me anymore. On the other hand, some organizations would see my age as an asset. It all depends on whether the age of a particular individual is deemed beneficial because of the *experience* it represents, or just an indication of a fossil better left alone. Interpretations vary.

One thing that might hurt me is the image—or lack thereof—that I project on the field. I've always wondered about this. I talked to John Boles about it earlier in the year, and although he really had no answer, he certainly understood what I was saying. Many managers, coaches, and baseball people like athletes with some demonstrative flair. That doesn't mean they want everybody to be "The Mad Hungarian" or even Tug McGraw, but a little emotion every now and then is well received. It's proof of the competitive fires burning inside. I enjoy watching emotionally charged athletes, too, as long as I'm convinced of their sincerity. Some ability to support the enthusiasm doesn't hurt, either. To make a short story shorter, I'm a very boring competitor to watch. I have no mannerisms, to my knowledge, which bring attention to myself. I don't jump up and down, offer high fives, or wear batting gloves as a fashion statement when I hit. Patty picked up on this years ago and has tried to get me to spruce up my act on the field. "Other guys pound their gloves," she says. "That wouldn't be so bad, would it? It would let people know you're alive."

She's right, but I've never been able to change. I can't help it and I have my father to thank for it. And I am thankful. My dad says more by saying less than anybody I know. He doesn't have an arrogant bone in his body and is exemplary of everything I'm drawn to in a man. I am what I am, to a large degree, because he's what he is. At least I hope that's why. The fact that I'm content with my demeanor doesn't necessarily mean it's all that convincing to my superiors, though. It's often misinterpreted as passiveness or as a telltale sign that I lack the old killer instinct. Joe Kerrigan told me recently that his opinion of me is exactly the opposite of what it was in spring training. "I thought you were soft," he said. "And regardless of what you hear later, first impressions are difficult to change. I thought you acted like you were having a job handed to you." Nothing could have been further from the truth, but I understood that his logic was based on sheer body language. This kind of thing may or may not have hindered my progress over the years. I'll never know.

Back in '79 when I was at instructional league with the Padres, all of us prospects were assembled in a classroom one night and issued a test. Its purpose was to determine the competitiveness within each individual. I received the highest score. I doubt that anyone put much stock in the test results. As a coach, I'd have a hard time trusting the transferable qualities of a multiple-choice questionnaire onto the field. However, I also don't believe that a person's confidence or spiritedness can be determined solely by observation.

Let me put it this way. Suppose I feared I'd have a disappointing season this year, or even a mediocre one, and I felt I'd be unable to compete with the Howard Farmers and Chris Nabholzes. Or suppose I thought I'd be lucky to have *comparable* results with my teammates. Actually, what if there had been doubt in my mind, from the beginning, that I would pitch *better* than anyone on this staff? Would I have bothered keeping this journal? Would I have wasted my time scribbling on a piece of paper every day if I'd doubted my ability to back it up? Confidence, determination, or little-boy enthusiasm: none of it has to be displayed to be felt.

Friday, August 31
Nashville

We had our last road game of the season tonight. It was typical of too many others we've played: long and ugly in a losing cause. I took a workout on the side in preparation for my final start, which will either be Sunday or Monday, the last day of the season. Nashville and Buffalo are deadlocked in a pennant race, and we conclude our season with a three-game homestand against Buffalo. I think Tim and Joe's idea is to hold me back, and, if the situation allows it, make Buffalo beat me in the final game. To be honest, I couldn't care less who wins it or when I pitch. My shingles are getting worse by the day, and I'm not looking forward to dealing with them.

Today Tim told me there's still a chance I could go up, that nothing has been finalized. I don't even tell Patty what the latest scoop is anymore. It's better simply to leave her in a constant state of definite doubt than to raise and lower her expectations all the time. I don't keep things from her to protect her, but what's the sense of babbling on about it?

Paul Marak and Tim Birtsas, the last two pitchers I've opposed (and defeated), are both in the big leagues now. I don't have any problems with that. I'm not against another individual succeeding. It just reiterates what I wrote earlier: major league players are the best in the world, but they're not astonishingly better than the players a rung below them on the ladder. It's possible that while millions may watch these two pitchers on television during the next month, I'll be in Bryan looking for a job. I know that I can pitch with both of them. For that matter, I know I can *hit* both of them.

I'm not in a good mood right now. We're busing back to Indianapolis from Nashville, which should find us pulling into our stadium at 5 A.M. or so. I'm already tired because the shingles haven't allowed a sound night's sleep lately, and every time there's a nice-sized bump in the road, I jump out of my skin. I'm sick and tired of it all and I can't stand being like this. I hate hosting a pity party when my family can't attend.

September

Saturday, September 1
Indianapolis

Joe told me today that they'd leave it up to me as far as which game I wanted to pitch. With no hesitation, I chose tomorrow instead of Monday.

Patty was thinking about coming down for the last weekend, but she decided against it, all things considered. It'd only be for a couple days and we'd be cooped up in my motel room. I'll be home soon, either for the winter or for the rest of my life, depending upon the decisions we make. Plus, I think she feels that, right now, I'm better off alone. I have a lot on my mind, and as much as I hate to admit it, I'm irritable. The season is winding down, and I don't know if I'll be able to pitch tomorrow, if I'll get called up, or if I'll ever pitch again. Soon I'll be unemployed, not knowing whether I should seek a winter job or another career, with no solid leads on either. I have a new son at home who I probably ought to acquaint myself with and two boys who just assume Daddy will take care of them. I'd never want them to feel otherwise, but it's not that easy.

My world isn't falling apart; I'm just taking myself too seriously. As the final day draws near, I'm losing some of the perspective I've tried to have all season. It's what has kept me sane, or close to it, for so many years. You'd think I'd grab hold of it, now more than ever. I'm guilty of too much reliance on myself and not enough on God.

Sunday, September 2
Indianapolis

I saved my worst for last. I went six innings tonight and gave up four runs on eleven hits. I didn't walk anybody and struck out three. I also hit a batter. On purpose.

After Buffalo scored their final two runs off me in the fifth with a two-out double (their tenth hit on the evening), I'd had enough. I knew we weren't going to score four runs, I knew I was about done for the night, first base was open, and mostly I was just tired of getting knocked around. There was a lot of frustration to deal with. At the time, drilling somebody seemed the logical outlet. Since my control is reliable, I'm not prone to hitting batters by accident. I'm very selective of my victims, although tonight's was nothing personal. It was strictly situational. I don't even know the guy.

Some pitchers will hit batters on the first pitch. It's definitely less subtle and leaves little doubt as to the intentions behind it. Although sometimes I admire that kind of strong statement, it's not my chosen method. Tonight's was typical of the art-form approach I follow. The guy was a lefty, and Gil Reyes called for a fastball-away first pitch. I shook him off and then shook off a curve as well. Gil knows I never second-guess his calls unless I have a good reason. He figured out what my reason was before he offered me a third choice. I could see him smiling under his mask as he moved inside and called for a fastball. I hit the inside corner for strike one. We want the hitter to know we're not afraid to pitch him inside.

Gil and I work so well together that he took over from there. He called for another fastball inside, and I delivered one a foot off the plate to brush the hitter back. We want the hitter to think that we might try to get him out by just pounding him with fastballs inside.

The next pitch was the key. Gil called for a slider and set up on the outside corner of the plate. We didn't want to throw a strike with this pitch either. I spun a lazy slider toward the dish and missed outside. Now it's a hitter's count at two balls and one strike. The hitter will be aggressive and will more than likely stride into the ball looking for something to drive, especially when all his teammates have had so much fun at the plate all night. Gil called for another fastball inside, and I drilled him near his waist. We didn't care what he thought anymore.

After I was finished, trainer John Spinosa came up to the clubhouse to tend to my body. We were just about ready to put some ice on my arm when I realized I didn't need any. "My arm's got plenty of time to recover, John. It could be five months or maybe even a lifetime before I throw again."

We both chuckled and he went back to the dugout. I showered, dressed, and packed up all my gear. I called Patty from the clubhouse, and we talked quite a while, with very few words devoted to baseball. We're eager to be a family again. I'll return home to a lot of uncertainties, but I won't have to face them alone.

If I were going up to the major leagues, I'd be fired up. I don't think that's what is going to happen, though, and I have to adjust my optimism accordingly. My family isn't a bad alternative.

Monday, September 3
Bryan, Ohio

I have several friends on Buffalo's team, so I made a point to seek them out before tonight's finale and wish them well. I thought maybe they should have given me a going-away present since I came away with only one win in six starts this season

211

against them. I talked with Mark Ryal most of the time. Our paths have crossed several times since we played together for the White Sox in '85. He told me that early in the count, I was making a slight alteration in my delivery that let him know when I was going to throw a slider. I told him that if he considered himself such a good friend he should have told me a long time ago what I was doing. Mark just laughed and assured me that no one else on his team had picked up on it.

That proves two things. First, that Mark and I are close enough that he kept his information to himself. Secondly, it shows the little differences that make Mark the best hitter in the league.

He had something else to tell me. He said he thought Buffalo would like to have me next year.

Mike Billoni then came over and we chatted for quite a while. Mike is the vice president and general manager of the Buffalo Bisons. We've known each other since '85 as well. He and I talked about my future. He understands how I feel and suggested I take a few days off after the season to let my head clear. Then he'd like me to write him a letter detailing exactly what it is I'd like to do. Then he'll talk to Bob Rich, Jr., and we'll all take it from there.

Baseball wasn't the objective. I like the city of Buffalo, and it's conceivable that, through Mike and Bob, I might have a chance at a job there after my playing career ends. If I felt that pitching in Buffalo would in any way solidify that future for my family, and if Buffalo wanted me for next season, I'd definitely consider it. Mike asked if I would be opposed to moving away from Bryan and I said that although we like it there, I'm not dead-set against moving.

I then had to return to the dugout for the presentation of awards. I was most valuable player for the month of August and was also rewarded for having the lowest ERA on the team.

Big deal.

That's probably not the reaction I should have, but it's how I feel, at least for now. There'll come a day when I'll draw some enjoyment from these accomplishments. I don't expect it to be soon, though. All my plaques and trophies are stored in a box in the attic. I could clutter an entire room with them if I wanted to. When I won awards in high school or college, I was proud of them. When I get them now, it does little more than frustrate me. It's hardly the type of recognition I want anymore.

I quickly showered and got dressed for the game. I was supposed to be in the stands charting the pitches, but, after I changed and turned in my uniform, I discovered that the radar gun had been packed away. So I sat in the clubhouse during the game and talked with Dwight Lowry, who was in uniform but knew he wouldn't play. I have more respect for Dwight than anyone I've ever played with, and I'll miss him.

I made a couple trips out to the car and finished loading all my baseball junk. I went to the concession stand, bought Patty a sweatshirt, and called home to remind her to leave the door unlocked tonight. All the normal activities you'd picture a player doing during a game.

We won our last game and concluded the season a mere twenty-four games out of first. Everybody poured into the clubhouse. It's amazing how quickly players disperse at the end of the year. The good-byes are usually short. Guys shake hands while they pack their bags. I don't know how long it took for the clubhouse to empty. I was the first one out. I made the rounds, talking some with Scott, Jim Davins, Joe, Gomer, and Tim.

Few baseball good-byes are emotional. I'd venture to say that a fair share of them aren't even sincere, my own included. Over the duration of a year, I'll develop two or three real friendships and another dozen or so "Christmas card" friends.

I jumped in my car and took off for home. I don't know what I was more anxious to do: get home or leave Bush Stadium behind. It's not anything against the people there, and I'll have no specific memories that'll haunt me. It's what *didn't* happen. I worked my tail off, stayed relatively healthy, didn't make waves, and, above all, pitched as well as I ever have. Probably *better* than I ever have. Nothing happened except a return trip to Bryan in September. I have an overabundance of pride, just like everyone else. This hurts. A lot.

It's now closing in on 4 A.M., and my family is fast asleep. It feels good to be home, yet I'm upset about it. Another season, possibly my last season, is over. All I can do in response to it is go to bed mad.

Monday, September 10
Bryan, Ohio

It's been a week now since the season ended. I'm adjusting to being home just fine. I still get upset when I think about this past year, but the frequency of those moments is already decreasing. I finished the season second in the league in ERA:

PITCHING TOP 10

PITCHER	CLUB	W—L	ERA	IP	H	BB	SO
Hammond, Chris	NVL	15–1	2.17	149	118	63	149
Fireovid, Steve	IND	10–12	2.63	171	163	34	84
Olivares, Omar	LOU	10–11	2.82	159	127	59	88
Taylor, Dorn	BUF	14–6	3.02	188	165	49	108
Lemasters, Jim	OMA	11–10	3.16	154	170	55	86
Gakeler, Dan	IND	5–5	3.23	120	101	55	89
Gross, Kip	NVL	12–7	3.27	127	112	46	62
Hinkle, Mike	LOU	8–7	3.29	129	126	40	66
Anderson, Scott	IND	12–10	3.31	182	166	61	116
Lopez, Rob	LOU	7–10	3.38	144	141	50	76

In some respects this was the best season I ever had. Since I'm always around the plate, I'm prone to surrendering a lot of hits. I've never been one to serve up a ton of home runs, or even extra-base hits, for that matter. That leaves singles and walks to do most of the damage. My walk ratio, again this year, was excellent. I walked one batter for every five innings pitched, which obviously averages out to fewer than two per nine innings. Although I'm by no means a strikeout pitcher, my ratio of strikeouts to walks was well above two to one. I was the only one on our staff to match that proportion, and, as you can see by looking at the pitchers listed above, I was one of the few in the league to accomplish it.

All players like to finish the season strong. August is probably the prime month to get hot, for a number of reasons: call-ups, job security for the following season, trade bait for other clubs, and just the overall morale of the athlete to know he executed well when so many others blatantly lay down. Here's what I did in August.

W—L	ERA	IP	H	BB	K		
3–2	2.04	44	29	5	25	*	two shutouts

In a nutshell, I'm pleased with the year I had. I would have liked more wins, but my won-lost record isn't indicative of how I threw. I can say I'm pleased, but it's a very short-lived pleasure I experience. Whatever it was I accomplished, it wasn't enough, at least not for the Expos. I have no doubts that I could have helped them. Manager Buck Rodgers, who wouldn't know me if I came up and bit him, and general manager Dave Dombrowski thought otherwise.

Life goes on.

A couple days ago, as I was unpacking my baseball gear, I came across an envelope stuffed inside my bag. I'd never opened it before because I knew what it was: it's a letter from the Expos notifying me of my free agency, effective October 15. The last couple years, I'd stopped really reading these letters, but this year, for some reason, I did. It appeared to be no different from the others I remembered from a more distant past. Except that it started out, "Dear Jeff."

I don't even think there was a Jeff on our team. I showed Patty.

"That's fitting," she said.

My agent, Jim Bronner, called today. He had just spoken with Dombrowski about me. Dave indicated he has no serious interest in me at the major league level for next season. Jim asked for my release now, rather than on October 15, so he could contact other clubs who might possibly want me right now. Perhaps there'd have been no interest anyway, but we'll never know. Dave wouldn't issue my release, saying he didn't want to set a precedent. Jim then asked if he could just talk to other teams to see if there was indeed any current interest in me. Dave responded with the same answer for the same reason. Jim's final proposal was to give Dave a list of clubs whom he felt might be interested in me and request that Dave make some calls himself. Dave said it would be a waste of time.

I know Dave has his grounds for not cooperating and that he couldn't care less about somebody he has no plans for. I also know what the word "understanding" means, not to be confused with "sympathetic." Dave chose to deal with his policies instead of his people. That's a shame, not a precedent. What could have happened if Dave had given me my release now instead of in another month? He loses nothing, either for himself or the organization. He doesn't want to be approached by other players or agents in the future under similar circumstances and have to answer to requests such as Jim's. By always saying no, he has no asterisks to hide.

First of all, my situation is far from common. Secondly, if word somehow leaked out about Dave granting such a wish, how many players would have reason to ask for such a release from him? Very few. Finally, if players within the organization *were* aware of some flexibility, they might view Dave as approachable. Maybe he doesn't want that. I should add that Jim had no problems at all in receiving a positive response to the same request for another player in a different organization.

In all fairness to Dave, I'll admit to having a limited understanding of front-office procedure. In this particular instance, though, I believe Dave portrayed an even lesser understanding of players and the careers we attempt to enhance, however a "waste of time" they may be.

On a much brighter subject, my family is great. The boys are busy, and for a while Patty and I are trying not to be. The

216

first couple weeks is always a period of adjustment around the house. Baseball forces Patty to be the man *and* woman of the home much of the time, and there's some surrendering of power that takes place with her. It's not an ego thing. It's finding or relocating that cohesiveness between us that enables us to be productive and contented parents. While she's letting go of some responsibilities, I'm trying to find my place in the unit. It's not nearly as complicated as it sounds, especially when we're both aware of what's going on. The boys are glad to have Dad around again.

Thursday, September 20
Bryan, Ohio

Since my season finished, Montreal called up a couple more pitchers, neither of whom were me. They reached down to Double-A and brought up lefthander Brian Barnes, a prospect who had a terrific year in Jacksonville.

And they called up Scott, too. Sometimes the good guys do win.

Speaking of good guys, Chris Nabholz, 0–6 with us, is, as of last night, 6–0 with the Expos.

I took a job with the Bryan Parks and Recreation Department again this fall, and this time I might stay past when it gets too cold to plant trees. Still, I've spent the past couple weeks talking to some people concerning career-type employment. So far, no long-term plans. Everything depends on what's available and whether I pitch again next year.

At the moment, I'm not leaning one way or the other. As far as baseball goes, I won't know how much interest there is, if any, until October 22, the earliest date other teams are allowed to contact free agents.

I do know that I'm not kidding myself about getting back to the majors. I just have to find the right team—like Dan Boone did this year. Dan was a teammate of mine with the Padres back in '81. Now he's thirty-six years old: three years older than me. He hadn't been in the majors since '82, and he'd been out of baseball altogether for a few years. Last year, he pitched in the new senior league. The Orioles signed him to a Triple-A contract. He had a terrific year in Rochester, but no better a year than I did. The Orioles called him up five days ago, and Dan's pitched well so far.

But I can't sit around until October 22, then make a decision. I'll stay with Parks and Rec, and, probably sometime in November, I'll figure out what to do.

If I choose to retire from ball, I'll look for a real job real hard. If I pitch again, I'm already set for winter work. I want to be committed one way or the other as soon as possible, but there's no way I can decide until I have a chance to consider the options.

My agent is confident there will be teams interested in me. If he's correct we'll evaluate the offers in terms of opportunity, money, and location. If he's wrong there's no decision to make. I think I had a good enough year to attract *some* curiosity. It's silly to speculate what will come my way, though. I've learned better.

More than likely, I'll be able to play baseball again next season if I want to. Patty and I both take some comfort in knowing that. She refers to it as our "safety net." It's apparent at this stage in my life that baseball will never provide lasting financial security, or some of the other dividends received by so many of my friends. There are two ways I can react to this. I can feel sorry for myself and hope others adopt the same pitiful opinion of me. Initially that'd be much easier and it's been inviting at different times during my career. Before long I'd have a contagious chip on my shoulder that would infect all other areas of my life. I can't do that. I wasn't put on this earth to be a bitter soul. The alternative thought process is to carry on and do my best. I have four others under this roof who should serve as more than enough motivation if I'm too delicate to supply it myself.

Perhaps, in my case, baseball is its own reward. I enjoy the game, and to still have the opportunity to pitch is in itself an honor. Naturally I want more. Donald Trump wants more. We *all* want more. I am blessed, however, with the ability to perform in an occupation that excites me. Not many people can say that, and by losing that perspective, I'd be degrading myself to a level already inhabited by far too many people, especially athletes. I can't and won't do that. Nobody owes me anything. We all have a choice in life. We can become possessed by those things we do not possess, or be grateful for the true blessings already received.

Epilogue

As the cold of winter approached, Steve Fireovid, along with his wife Patty, decided to give his pitching career one last shot in the spring of 1991. After leaving the Expos organization as a free agent on October 16, Fireovid was pleased when, just a day later, the Pittsburgh Pirates called to express interest in him. Apparently the Pirates remembered very well how solidly Fireovid had pitched against Pittsburgh's Triple-A franchise in Buffalo.

Within a few days, the Bucs offered Fireovid a contract to report to their spring training site in Bradenton, Florida in February, 1991. Steve was told he would receive an opportunity to make the Pirates' major league club.

Fireovid insists that he's optimistic yet realistic about his chances with the Pirates. Yet no matter how one views the situation, this simple fact sticks in Steve's heart: "I'm a professional pitcher, and I do this job well."

Index

INDEX

Earned run average, 45, 53, 54,
65, 77, 86, 90–91, 106, 112,
138, 139, 163, 168, 169, 177,
179, 189, 212, 214, 215
Elia, Lee, 162
Embarrassment, 119–120
Enthusiasm, on-field, 203–204
Errors, 52, 87, 105, 162, 189
ESPN, 51, 71, 154
Estrada, Chuck, 119
Extra innings, 52, 85

Family, 39, 82, 96–97, 100–101,
118, 136, 146–151, 156–157,
160, 194–196, 216–217
Famous Chicken, 108–109
Fans, 78, 108–109, 132, 143–
144, 191
Farmer, Howard, 36, 38, 47, 51,
52, 56, 66, 73, 75, 76–77, 88,
89, 90, 97, 98–99, 105, 108,
112, 123, 131–132, 140, 153–
154, 162, 201–202
Fastball, 11, 12, 26–27, 52, 68,
78, 79, 102, 104, 121, 144,
148, 171, 177, 196, 210, 211
Fatigue, late-season, 192
Field coordinators, 6
Fielding practice, 74
Filson, Pete, 112
First basemen, 44
First outings, 17–18
Florida State League, 34
Food, 8, 27, 79, 80, 109, 110,
115, 126, 197
Forkball, 53, 66
40-man roster, 10–11, 190
Free agency, 6, 183, 215–217
Frey, Jim, 88, 106
Friendships, 19, 174–175, 191–
192, 213
Fun, 71, 82, 86, 91

Gakeler, Dan, 112, 120, 178, 214
Gammons, Peter, 51, 88, 99
General managers, 79, 212, 215

Giannoulas, Ted, 108–109
Gilhooley, Bob, 88
Goff, Jerry, 37, 72, 73, 101
Grimsley, Roger, 168
Grissom, Marquis, 51
Gross, Kevin, 172, 174
Gross, Kip, 214
Ground balls, 31, 63, 68, 103,
108
Grounds crew, 36, 96
Gwynn, Tony, 84, 138–139

Hall of Fame, 138, 144
Hammond, Chris, 112, 214
Hartenstein, Chuck, 11
Hawaii, 10, 12, 86, 141
Hayes, Von, 142
Hesketh, Joe, 54
High school baseball, 90, 116, 213
Hill, Ken, 71, 112
Hinkle, Mike, 112, 214
Hit batters, 137, 210
Hitting instructors, 33
Hodge, Gomer, 85
Home openers, 42
Home-plate umpires, 137, 200–
201
Home runs, 155
Honolulu, Hawaii, 141
Hotels and motels, 7, 39, 41, 115
Hot weather, 129, 135

Independent teams, 34–35
Indianapolis, Ind., 40–49, 55–57,
64–70, 76–84, 90–91, 95–99,
107–117, 132–135, 140–146,
148, 151–161, 175–177, 181–
188, 192–196, 209–211
Indianapolis Indians, 17, 22, 27,
28, 40–49, 67, 137
Injuries, 22, 37, 44, 45, 71, 77,
85, 103, 137–138, 156, 167–
168, 170
Instructional league, 99, 204
Iowa Cubs, 28, 36, 126
Italian baseball, 130–131, 176

225

Roster expansion, 16, 33, 190
Roster reduction, 54, 57, 64, 71,
    82–83, 87, 90
Runnels, Tom, 32
Running, 110, 135–136, 157
Ryal, Mark, 212

Saberhagen, Brett, 4
St. Laurent, Jim, 45–46, 57
St. Louis Cardinals, 71
Salaries, 57, 154
Salazar, Angel, 115
San Diego Padres, 10, 12, 14, 32,
    50, 81, 86, 89, 119, 132–133,
    138–139, 141, 143–144, 204
San Juan Metros, 142
Santovenia, Nelson, 101
Schmidt, Dave, 159
Schuerholz, John, 4
Schumaker, Max, 42
Scouts, 50, 65, 75
Scranton, Pa., 87–90
Scudder, Scott, 112
Seattle Mariners, 81, 167–170
Sherry, Norm, 13, 14
Show, Eric, 142
Shutouts, 44, 55, 80, 200, 215
Sinatro, Matt, 142
Sinker, 200
Skinner, Joel, 97
Slider, 11, 13, 19, 26–27, 102,
    129, 171, 177, 188–189, 196,
    211, 212
Slumps, 63–64, 72, 78, 79–80
Smith, Bryn, 6
Smith, Steve, 50
Smith, Zane, 177, 185
Southern League, 107
Spinosa, John, 25, 27, 124, 178,
    198, 211
Split-finger fastball, 125, 129
Sporting News, 13–14
Springsteen, Bruce, 175
Spring training, 5–34, 89, 170
Stanicek, Steve, 88
Statistics, 77, 86, 90–91, 112–
    113, 138–139, 179, 214, 215

Steels, James, 32–33, 37, 45, 85
Steiner, Charlie, 154–155
Stewart, Dave, 79–80
Stone, Steve, 174
Straker, Les, 61
Strikeouts, 18, 19, 40, 63, 117,
    129, 144, 214–215
Strike zone, 137, 201
Superstars, 132–133
Syracuse, N.Y., 81, 84, 167–173

Taylor, Dorn, 112, 214
Team meetings, 70–71, 79–80,
    107–108, 136–137
Tempe, Ariz., 167, 170
Tenace, Gene, 119–120
Terrell, Walt, 142
Texas League, 41
Texas Rangers, 174
Thompson, Rich, 64–65, 72
Thurmond, Mark, 10–11
Tidewater, Va., 196–200
Toledo, Ohio, 100, 118, 121–124
Toronto Blue Jays, 4, 49, 83, 170
Torve, Kelvin, 19
Trades, 79, 89, 90, 139, 157,
    177, 185, 215
Trainers, 25–26, 168, 198
Travel, 9, 16, 37, 41, 49–50, 70,
    75, 84, 87, 98, 115, 120–121,
    124, 126, 135, 152–153, 160
Triple-A baseball, 5, 10–11, 12,
    23, 28, 34, 37, 49, 50, 71, 84,
    86, 90, 106, 138, 139, 141,
    167, 170, 183, 185, 191, 218

Umpires, 35, 38, 96, 137, 200–
    201
Uniforms, 20–21, 25, 27, 42–43,
    119
Unwinding after games, 85–86

Valle, Dave, 97
Van Poppel, Todd, 154
Velocity of pitches, 46, 65, 68, 73,
    79, 98–99, 117, 129, 132–133,
    148